A GUIDE TO BUILDING

EDUCATION PARTNERSHIPS

# A GUIDE TO BUILDING EDUCATION PARTNERSHIPS

### Navigating Diverse Cultural Contexts to Turn Challenge Into Promise

*Matthew T. Hora and Susan B. Millar*

Foreword by Judith Ramaley

1996–2011 15TH ANNIVERSARY

Stylus
PUBLISHING, LLC.

STERLING, VIRGINIA

Published by Stylus Publishing, LLC
22883 Quicksilver Drive
Sterling, Virginia 20166-2102

Library of Congress Cataloging-in-Publication-Data
Hora, Matthew T., 1972-
    A guide to building education partnerships : navigating
diverse cultural contexts to turn challenge into promise /
Matthew T. Hora and Susan B. Millar ; foreword by Judith
Ramaley.—1st ed.
       p.   cm.
    Includes bibliographical references and index.
    ISBN 978-1-57922-472-1 (pbk. : alk. paper)
    ISBN 978-1-57922-489-9 (library networkable e-edition)
    ISBN 978-1-57922-490-5 (consumer e-edition)
 1. Educators—United States—Professional relationships.
 2. College-school cooperation—United States.
 3. Government aid to education—United States.
 4. Business and education—United States.
 5. Interorganizational relations—United States.
 I. Millar, Susan Bolyard.   II. Title.
LB1775.2.H67   2011
371.19—dc22
                                                    2010031556


13-digit ISBN: 978-1-57922-472-1 (paper)
13-digit ISBN: 978-1-57922-489-9 (library networkable
e-edition)
13-digit ISBN: 978-1-57922-490-5 (consumer e-edition)

Printed in the United States of America

Bulk Purchases

Quantity discounts are available for use in workshops
and for staff development.
Call 1-800-232-0223

First Edition, 2011

10   9   8   7   6   5   4   3   2   1

# CONTENTS

# ACKNOWLEDGMENTS

We acknowledge with gratitude the funding agency whose support enabled production of this book. We also acknowledge those partnership researchers whose work we found invaluable in writing this book and whose insights have fared well over the years. First, Naida Tushnet's research on forming educational partnerships was an incredibly valuable resource and demonstrated how to translate theory into action. Second, Barbara Intriligator's work on identifying the appropriate structures for partnership provided a key insight into our research. Third, Sirotnik and Goodlad's seminal book on school-university partnerships set the stage for avoiding one-size-fits-all solutions to the challenges facing education in the United States.

We heartily thank the researchers who conducted the analyses during 2009 that informed this book; each of them spent countless hours analyzing transcripts and coding and analyzing data. We also thank the researchers and evaluators who worked on the Urban District Education Partnership (UDEP) project. They provided valuable constructive criticism, scores of references to useful books or articles, and feedback that helped us conceptualize this book. To maintain the anonymity of the partnership described in this book, we cannot name these dedicated individuals, but you know who you are. To all of the teachers, faculty, administrators, and UDEP staff who patiently sat through our interviews over the course of five years, we deeply appreciate the time and insights you shared with us. We thank John von Knorring, president of Stylus Publishing, for his extraordinary support and involvement in the development of this book. We also owe a debt of gratitude to the many reviewers of the book's preliminary draft, who provided insightful critiques and suggestions for improving the manuscript. Of these reviewers, we especially thank Judith Ramaley, who graciously provided the foreword to this book.

In addition, we each thank a separate set of individuals. *Matthew*: I thank Susan Millar for her mentorship, and Rich Halverson and Michael Paolisso for introducing me to research on systems of practice and cognitive anthropology, respectively, and for their support and encouragement over the years. *Susan*: I thank Matthew Hora for taking on the challenge of first-authoring this book, Elaine Seymour for her friendship and insights into the book-writing process, and Sangtae Kim for his support during 2009–2010.

# FOREWORD

Throughout my years of trying to create partnerships that really work, I have focused time and time again on one vital question: How can educators close the gaps that separate theory, policy, and practice and that limit our ability to implement what we have learned in ways that will help students succeed? *A Guide to Building Education Partnerships* helps to answer that question in a straightforward and workable fashion. It makes sense to scholars, policy makers, and practitioners; I know because I tested it.

After I reviewed an initial draft of this book, I realized that it offers clear and usable lessons for anyone trying to put together real collaborations in the untidy world of policy and practice. It helped me crystallize fleeting insights I have had in the course of years of practical experience about how to create fruitful working relationships among diverse partners. I thus wrote to the authors, asking permission to use the document as a starting point for a conversation with the Minnesota Commissioner of Education Alice Seagren and several of her senior colleagues. "Maybe we could beta test it for you," I wrote hopefully, "and show whether this overall perspective applies to a very different kind of education partnership and a different set of partners."

My goal was to sit down with Dr. Seagren and map out the environment in which our state, Minnesota, was attempting to address disparities in student achievement. Using only the overview provided in the introduction to this book, we were able to create a "user's guide to educational reform in Minnesota." The conceptual framework offered in this book was exactly what we needed. We talked about the individual psychology and cultures of each major participant (institutes of higher education, the Minnesota Department of Education, school districts, the Minnesota Board of Teaching, and the teachers' union) as well as the educators, staff members, administrators, parents, and communities that create the settings in which our reform efforts play out. We discussed not only how we think about our work but also the places in which we do that work. We explored how we might build what the authors call the "3rd space of partnership," where people come together to invent the relationships and deploy the ideas and tools that make the most sense for them. We began to create a 3rd space in which we could work together differently and identify, manage, and reconcile "competing interests, perspectives, and opinions," all of which deserve attention and all of which may offer much-needed insights.

As Dr. Seagren and I talked that afternoon, and sketched circles and boxes on a whiteboard in the commissioner's office, we began to understand our environment in new ways. The hurdles became clear. The policy-making life cycle tends to be short—usually two, four, or six years. Given their often brief terms of office, legislators and school principals and superintendents do not have much time to put their ideas into action, so they need quick and convincing results to persuade their boards or colleagues to support the changes they are trying to make. The reform life cycle is much longer—usually, a decade or more must pass before it becomes clear whether a particular set of interventions will work. Some schools will have experienced leadership turnover several times during one decade, and many teachers who entered the profession with such hope and promise will have left for jobs in other districts or even other fields. In addition, students will have been swept into what some educators call "the churn," moving frequently from one school to another and from one curriculum approach to another. Educators are working in unstable systems that we sometimes disrupt further with our well-meaning efforts at reform. Finally, we have too many participants, too many conflicting goals, too many standards, and too many topics to cover.

What makes *A Guide to Building Education Partnerships* so helpful is that it provides a robust conceptual framework for taking into account pre-existing conditions such as these in order to build a successful 3rd space of partnership. By drawing on evidence from various disciplines, the authors have created a practical and well-grounded guide to creating and learning in a collaborative mode. Whatever else this 3rd space may represent, it always is a learning space, a shared workbench, and a gathering place where people can learn together in new ways, work together differently, and record and make sense of the experiences they share as they gradually move through the natural phases of working together on common goals.

In my own experience, collaboration seems to go through some of the same phases as any other maturing relationship. Individuals peer at each other across a no-person's-land of differences and puzzle over what they see. Then they begin to talk. If we educators follow the advice in this book, we will take enough time to explore the resources we bring to a collaboration, the experiences we have had, and the important similarities and differences in the larger landscape each of us knows so well. It is important to realize that the structural features and tasks—organizing the partnership and beginning to develop policies, procedures, and tasks—are not the real work of collaboration. Rather, they are the means to a very important goal: to allow people to get to know each other, to develop mutual respect, to agree on what a successful result will look like, and how to chart the path ahead. Educators are, as the subtitle of this guide proclaims, "navigating diverse cultural contexts." If we pay attention to relationships and the realities of our diverse backgrounds and experiences, we will "turn challenge into promise" and create a powerful synergy among different players in our educational system.

Fresh from that productive Minnesota afternoon that was shaped by *A Guide to Building Education Partnerships*, I offer the following suggestions for you when you read this book. First, think about how these insights might work in your own organization and environment and how they may be applied to your own imperatives, demands, and reform efforts. Second, consider whether you have given enough time and attention to the most important asset of all, namely, what each of your current or potential partners brings to this work—the insights and values of your respective cultures, your sense of shared purpose, and the wisdom that has come from your diverse experiences and practices.

Judith Ramaley
President, Winona State University

# INTRODUCTION

## The Challenge and Promise of Education Partnerships

Chances are that if you are reading this book you are, or soon will be, involved in a cross-organizational partnership intended to improve education. If so, you are part of a groundswell of interest in education partnerships as a solution to the complex and entrenched challenges facing education in the United States and abroad. In the United States, these challenges include low international standing in math and science achievement, teacher-training programs and processes that need improvement, misalignment between curricula taught in K–12 schools and curricula of institutions of higher education (IHEs), and the need to improve access to college for at-risk and underrepresented individuals. Because no single organization can solve these problems alone, practitioners need the skills and assets of multiple organizations and individuals and thus must collaborate across institutions, authority lines, organizational and cultural boundaries, and funding sources.

Indeed, the partnership strategy is currently a core part of U.S. federal education policy. For instance, the U.S. Department of Education's Math and Science Partnership program is intended to improve student achievement in math and science by partnering high-need K–12 districts with IHE faculty, businesses, and nonprofit organizations. Private funders are also promoting partnerships as a strategy to effect systemic reform in the U.S. educational system. For example, the Carnegie Corporation of New York, the Annenberg Foundation, and the Ford Foundation jointly sponsor the Teachers for a New Era project to strengthen teaching in K–12 districts by improving teacher-training programs at IHE schools of education. More than 20 years ago, in comments on partnerships between schools and universities when private foundations were beginning to support the partnership move-ment, John Goodlad (Sirotnik & Goodlad, 1988) said that "advocacy of school-university partnerships is *de rigeur*, and not to have one or be part of one could be dangerous to your educational health" (p. 103). In 2010, this sentiment is deeply entrenched in both policy and research and extends beyond school-university partnerships to include schools' collaboration with state and local governments, nonprofit organizations, and the business sector.

Despite these high expectations, participants often find it difficult to design and manage education partnerships and simultaneously obtain com-pelling evidence that they are actually achieving their goals. This holds true of partnerships in the business world as well: a 1999 study by the firm Accenture (1999) found that although 82% of executives felt that partner-ships were a prime vehicle for growth in a globalized economy, only 39% of partnerships met their expectations. If you talk to almost any administrator who has tried to manage a partnership, you will learn that designing and implementing partnerships is a taxing venture. Challenges associated with partnerships include aggressive timelines, demonstration of program efficacy, securing of funding and resources, and scalability. In particular, those involved in education partnerships will likely have tales to tell about how hard it is to navigate the different organizational structures, behavioral norms, and daily practices that distinguish K–12 schools from higher educa-tion institutions, and one academic discipline from another.

That said, based on decades of research on collaborative work in edu-cation, business, and health care, we do know something about the key ingredients that can make partnerships effective. For instance, research on professional-development schools indicates that collaborative decision-making systems that actively involve representatives from the community and participating K–12 districts and IHEs are key to creating and sustain-ing effective partnerships. However, the literature on education partner-ships tends to ignore research from fields such as administrative and organization science, which severely limits the evidence base on which to draw. Furthermore, research on partnerships in education often derives best practices from single cases, which may or may not translate to the unique conditions and contexts of a particular school, district, or IHE. These best practices, offered as a recipe for partnership success, tend to be insufficiently context sensitive and fail to open the black box of partnership operations to reveal the operational mechanisms by which partnership activities lead to particular outcomes.

No football coach would take a playbook designed for one team and mechanically apply it to a team with different players, skills, and competitors. As Peter Senge (1994) says, the common procedure of presenting the best practices of successful efforts "can do more harm than good, leading to piecemeal copying and playing catch-up" (p. 11). He advises that leaders' energies are better spent studying the principles of disciplines that underlie successful management. This is also true for partnership work, which takes a variety of forms, from complex arrangements between schools and universities fostered by government-funded projects, to small working groups comprising different departmental representatives within a single university. As education researcher Marilyn Johnston (1997) says, "Partnership is an untidy business, full of uncharted territories, ambiguities, and institutional complexities" (p. 1). A one-size-fits-all proscriptive approach to partnerships is likely doomed to fail, as it ignores or conceals the innumerable local variations and contextual factors that shape how a given partnership will look. Further complicating partnership work is the fact that each of us brings his or her own models of the world to the table.

So it is that teachers and administrators from both the K–12 and IHE sectors are largely left to their own devices and experiences when it comes to designing and managing partnerships tailored to their own unique situations. With so many resources and hopes devoted to partnerships and the increasing need to cooperate across organizational boundaries, the stakes are high. We educators need to learn from the successes and mistakes of people in all sectors who have engaged in partnership work over the decades. Educators and researchers owe it to our students, our colleagues, taxpayers, and ourselves to get it right.

We wrote this book to help fill the gaps in the partnership literature and to provide a road map to help K–12 and IHE practitioners, program administrators, and policy makers navigate the twists and turns of partnership. This book is based on a review of research literature from a variety of fields (e.g., education, management, anthropology) and an analysis of a five-year-long, publicly funded partnership. Our intent is to provide educators who are considering becoming, or are already, involved in partnerships with the diagnostic tools to undertake a deliberate and research-based approach to planning, designing, and managing a partnership.

This book does not provide a magic bullet that will work in all partnership situations: there is no one right way. While we eschew a one-size-fits-all model, our review of empirical research on both successful and unsuccessful partnerships revealed common principles. We discovered that successful and effective partnerships share certain practices and principles at specific stages. These principles form the core of the book. When presenting our principles, we do not minimize the conflicts and complexities inherent in partnership work; to do so would be to present coherence and homogeneity where they do not exist. Instead, we believe that it is these very organizational and cultural differences that give partnerships their promise. Indeed, the principles for planning and implementing education partnerships that we present here are built on a diagnosis of these differences and include sets of strategies for working with and through these differences.

We also identify several questions that are important to attend to and that this book can help you address:

- Why engage in a partnership?
- How do you select the best organizational structure and procedures for a partnership?
- How can you work with school and university leaders and teachers to design and manage effective partnerships?
- How can you foster meaningful interactions and collaborations among K–12, higher education, and other partners?
- How can you maintain open, deliberative discussion while respecting different histories and cultures?
- How can you communicate the potential benefits of partnership to motivate teachers, faculty, administrators, and community members?
- How can you produce compelling evidence that the partnership is worthwhile?

Even as better research and recommendations—such as those we hope you will find here—become available, partnership leaders often are forced to operate in completely uncharted territory. In such situations, you should expect many missteps and failures and should regard these negative outcomes as useful navigation guides. The aphorism "Nothing ventured, nothing gained" holds in such circumstances. However, most of the problems that education partnerships address are well known, so most major failures should—and can—be avoided with careful planning and proactive management of the inevitable challenges and conflicts.

## The Nature of Education Partnerships

In the literature on education partnerships, the term "partnership" is defined in a variety of ways and used interchangeably with terms such as "collaboration." Some researchers do not define partnership at all, or they rely on a definition that compares it with other organizational forms such as collaborations. Thus, the term "partnership" is sometimes used as a catchall phrase to describe any sort of cooperative relationship, without delving into the nuances of the actual relationship. Because this lack of specificity does not advance our understanding of the education partnership phenomenon, we offer our own definition:

> A K–20 partnership is an organization (i.e., a social entity in which people routinely engage together in tasks) that is formed through an agreement among partners, comprising entities such as IHEs, K–12 school districts, and governmental agencies, and intended to accomplish benefits that the partners, alone, could not accomplish (Clifford & Millar, 2008).

## Why Do Education Partnerships Form?

In recent years, one reason for partnership formation has been the belief that because the educational system is interconnected, it is the responsibility of all educators—from pre-K through higher education—to be involved in systemic reform (Hodgkinson, 1999). In addition, partnerships form for a multitude of other reasons, which include necessity, legitimization, and reciprocity. (We elaborate on this research in chapter 2.) Most of these reasons boil down to the following: to achieve particular goals, different organizations and individuals need each other's diverse skills and assets. In times of economic austerity, some K–12 districts and IHEs join forces with other organizations to acquire valuable financial support or resources that enable them to pursue important educational goals. For example, the Georgia Early College Initiative was motivated by a commonly held view that underrepresented students (e.g., English-language learners) face an array of obstacles to obtaining college degrees. The Bill and Melinda Gates Foundation and the Robert W. Woodruff Foundation provided funding to the University System of Georgia to establish "early college schools," where students can earn a high school diploma under personalized supervision while acquiring credits applicable to local IHEs. This effort involves the active engagement of a local K–12 district, an IHE, and the local community, all of which are the joint recipients of grants to create the early college schools. While this is but one example of the rationale for forming a partnership, a common thread in many initiatives is the need to acquire resources and to improve access to high-quality education for all students, particularly at-risk and underrepresented students.

However, motivations for forming partnerships are not limited to these publicly stated reasons. Most organizations also have in mind some degree of self-interest, such as increased legitimacy or status in the field, or access to particular decision-making agencies or individuals. In addition, individuals in K–12 schools and IHEs have their own motivations for participating, which may range from altruism to a desire to influence local educational policy. Knowing about the nature of the motivations guiding each of your potential partners, both organizations and individuals, will improve your capacity to initiate and implement successful partnerships. For example, you should be cautious about proceeding with partners who are motivated by too much or too little self-interest. Organizations that are motivated to advance both their own interests and the lives and interests of other entities and individuals, such as a K–12 district or a city's population as a whole, are likely to make the best partners.

## *Who Initiates Education Partnerships?*

Education partnerships are initiated by agents that are either external or internal to a school or university, and sometimes by a combination of both. Many partnerships are instigated internally by individual teachers or administrators who identify a challenge or problem and the potential partners that could help achieve a mutually beneficial goal. In other cases, a government agency or private foundation establishes a funding program whose criteria include creating new partnerships, as in the case of the aforementioned Math and Science Partnership program, the Teachers for a New Era program, and the Early College Initiative. The term "policy-induced partnerships" refers to the situation in which national or state policy makers make grants available on a competitive basis for partnership projects (Kingsley, 2005). Motivated by the promise of funding, organizations that otherwise would not seek to collaborate may enter into an "arranged marriage." For example, the Urban District Education Partnership (UDEP), the partnership analyzed in this book, was "policy induced." The funding agency set up an open competition and invited proposals. In such cases, the external funding agency should be considered a partner in its own right, even if it takes a hands-off approach to the day-to-day operations of the work. Other initiators of partnerships include businesses and policy think tanks, which promote collaborative work for a variety of reasons.

## Key Differences Among Partner Organizations

Education partnerships may involve many different types of "home" organizations, by which we mean the organizations to which the people involved in a partnership report or primarily belong. The most common home organizations are a subset or all of a K–12 district and a subset or all of an IHE (whether a community college, baccalaureate and master's degree–granting college, or research university). Many of these comprise just one department in a K–12 school or one or more higher education faculty members, whereas others are made up of an entire school district or a whole university. Education partnerships may also involve different types of IHEs, such as a network of community colleges and a research university, or different departments (e.g., mathematics and mathematics education) within a university. Thus, a core difference among organizations in education partnerships has to do with the unique histories, traditions, governance structures, and missions of K–12 schools and IHEs. Considering that many partnerships also involve government agencies and businesses, several different types of organizations may be represented in a partnership.

Disciplinary affiliation and identity constitute another point of distinction within partnerships. In some cases, identification with a particular K–12 school or IHE may be secondary to teachers' identification with their own department or discipline. For example, one Teachers for a New Era project brought together faculty from an IHE's mathematics, biology, and education departments, and bridging these different areas of expertise and forging a common sense of identity proved to be quite challenging. Each difference constitutes a boundary between people and groups that needs to be crossed effectively for a partnership to succeed.

## Education Partnership Types

It is important to understand that there are several recognized types of partnership structures. Based on the literature, we suggest that education partnerships can be understood as a variation on one of three distinct organizational types. The three types are "limited" partnerships, in which one organization clearly directs the actions of others; "coordinated" partnerships, which involve horizontal coordination but no centralized governance; and "collaborative" partnerships, in which partners are tightly coupled and employ a consensus-based governance system. These organizational types should be thought of on a continuum, with limited and collaborative types representing the highest and lowest degree of organizational autonomy, the greatest and least degree of hierarchical governance systems, and so forth. (We elaborate on this in chapter 5.) It is also important to note that within a single partnership, different structures may be used for different levels of the organization. For instance, the partnership as a whole may be organized as a collaborative entity, but smaller working groups engaged in the specific work can be organized as limited partnerships.

The collaborative type of partnership deserves special attention. Barbara Gray (1989) captured the core idea that distinguishes this type of arrangement when she wrote, "Collaboration is a process through which parties who see different aspects of a problem can constructively explore their differences and search for solutions that go beyond their own limited vision of what is possible" (p. 5). It is this potential for constructive exploration of differences and development of solutions that makes collaborative partnerships so attractive and yet so challenging at the same time. In fact, some researchers explicitly warn that collaborative partnerships are the most difficult to design and manage, and that although their successful implementation can yield impressive results, they are more likely to fail than succeed. This is important to bear in mind if you seek funding from federal and state organizations, which tend to expect their grantees to form partnerships of the most promising type, that is, collaborative. However, a successful limited or coordinative partnership may be more productive than a failed collaborative partnership.

Indeed, we recognize that not all situations call for a partnership, and that in some cases a partnership of any type may be unnecessary or untenable. We do not claim that partnerships are a panacea for all of the challenges facing education, and while we believe that they can be effective and even transformative if done well, they can also be frustrating and ineffective. It is up to you to determine whether your particular situation calls for a partnership with another organization or individual. We hope that if you decide to go down the partnership path, this book will help you attain your goals.

## Working in a Partnership: New Tasks and Challenges

We wrote this book for the practitioners who design, manage, and implement partnerships. Thus, our target audience is not just superintendents, principals, deans, or principal investigators (if funded by a grant), but also the teachers, faculty, and program staff "on the ground" who will be engaged in the actual work of the partnership. However, we focus on those individuals who are involved in leadership roles at all levels of the partnership, as they will face unique tasks and challenges. As in organizations of any type, leadership in education partnerships is not limited to the one or two superintendents or superstar faculty members who act as the public face or champions of a partnership. While these leaders are undoubtedly important, leadership is distributed throughout organizations and encompasses all individuals, at all levels, who make decisions about management, tasks, resources, and vision. Thus, leaders run the gamut, from the principal investigators of a grant to the teachers who guide their students to experience new, powerful approaches to learning. Each represents one of the many facets of leadership in a partnership and, ideally, each effectively acts as both an administrator and a cultural broker for different audiences at different times.

In contrast to leaders within established organizations, leaders within partnerships also face the challenges of forming and guiding an especially complex quasiorganization. As you probably know all too well, schools and universities have policies and structures to handle different kinds of situations. For example, the human resources department handles personnel issues and conflicts, and the business or accounting office deals with fiscal issues. These policies and structures help not only to manage but also to shape organizational expectations and behaviors—for better or for worse. You and other individuals have probably developed "routine expertise," the skills and knowledge required to solve familiar problems competently when dealing with these policies and structures on a regular basis. However, in the more emergent and unpredictable environments in which partnerships operate, established policies and structures will not be at hand, and you will be faced with new situations and problems. This requires "adaptive expertise," the ability to apply your skills and knowledge to novel problems and situations that inevitably arise in partnership work. Of particular value for the unpredictable nature of partnerships is the ability of adaptive experts to use their knowledge to create new solutions for atypical cases or unique problems, instead of applying preexisting knowledge in the accustomed way. Moreover, leading an education partnership not only requires the managerial skill to set up workable structures and procedures, but also good communication skills and the ability to cross boundaries. Because this is no small challenge, we focus in this book on the role of leaders—at all levels—in designing and managing partnerships.

> Routine expertise refers to highly developed skills and knowledge that are applied to predictable, everyday problems. Partnership work requires you to use adaptive expertise and apply this knowledge to new situations and problems.

## Methodology: Understanding the Underlying Mechanisms of Partnership

The original research on which this book is based is a longitudinal and comparative case study of a project, called the UDEP. This project was part of a publicly funded program to improve math and science education for students in K–12 schools by establishing partnerships among STEM (science, technology, engineering, and mathematics) faculty, education faculty, and K–12 administrators and teachers. UDEP was funded for five years starting in 2003. Its primary aim was to improve mathematics and science teaching and learning in urban school districts by bringing about organizational changes in school districts and IHEs.

We used an embedded-case-study research design that enabled an in-depth analysis of the complex and subtle dynamics of organizational process within a partnership. An embedded case study focuses on multiple units of analysis; in this case we looked at the partnership as a whole and then focused on four distinct working groups within the larger partnership. A *working group* is a group that has responsibility for accomplishing a task intended to help achieve one or more of a partnership's goals, has at least two members who represent different organizations (or administrative units from the same organization), and meets at least three times to make progress on its tasks. We chose this approach because studies that consider a partnership as a whole without delving into the specific activities of subunits might obscure the specific and unique processes at work in different contexts. In using this approach, we captured different partnership processes as they unfolded in different contexts. This focus on process builds on existing research in organizational science on collaborations and interorganizational relations in which researchers have opened and investigated the black box of organizational process rather than focusing their analysis on inputs and outcomes. From the myriad working groups within the UDEP partnership, we chose to focus on the following four:

- The senior leadership group consisted of leaders from each of the partners and was given the task of providing overall management and vision for the entire project. This group became increasingly dysfunctional and eventually evolved into separate leadership teams centered at two of the IHEs.
- A preservice math group based in an IHE was a committee of faculty and doctoral students from the mathematics department and an education department at one of the IHEs and representatives from the local district.
- A science professional-development group based in a district consisted of education and science faculty from two local IHEs, representatives from the local district, and professional-development consultants from another IHE. The group focused on developing a series of science professional-development workshops for K–12 teachers in a large urban district.
- A math professional-development group based in a district consisted of the members of one district's math leadership team guided by leaders from one of the IHEs. This group began operating as part of a district/IHE initiative that had begun before the UDEP grant was funded.

Based on this study, we provided UDEP leaders with formative evaluation findings identifying what did and did not work and why. In so doing, we learned that the partnership leaders found most valuable information about the following questions: (1) Which structural and cultural features influenced partnership operations over time? (2) What were the characteristics of the newly formed partnership? (3) What were the key underlying principles for effective partnership management? We addressed these questions by tracking over a five-year period these and other working groups' formation, evolution, and final outcomes as they unfolded in their natural environment of school districts and universities. Although the UDEP project was unusual, particularly in size and scope, many of our key findings were echoed in the research literature in education, interorganizational relations, and collaboration, as well as in our personal experiences as program evaluators. The overlaps among these data types inform the principles of partnership that constitute the core of this book. (A more detailed discussion of our methodology appears in the appendix.) Finally, although we conducted a descriptive case study of the sort that we critiqued earlier, our approach differs from the usual in two important ways: (1) we focus not on describing the partnership as a whole but on specific components as they interact over time, and (2) we derive from our analysis a diagnostic framework for understanding cross-organizational partnerships instead of a list of best practices.

> The principles of partnership that form the core of this book are based on our case-study findings, the research literature, and our own experiences as program evaluators.

## Conceptual Framework

In introducing you to the conceptual framework that guides this book, we begin by explaining how our approach differs from much of the existing research on education partnerships. These other researchers tend to focus on *what* partnerships do, rather than *how* they operate or *why* participants do the things that they do. This approach does not explain why a particular initiative succeeds or fails, taking into account that schools and universities are complex organizations with many moving parts (Patton, 2006). For this reason, researchers and practitioners alike increasingly are turning to approaches that illuminate the processes or internal mechanisms of partnership. Compounding this problem is the issue that much of the partnership research is atheoretical and thus lacks the conceptual means to analyze the complex interactions among individuals, groups, and organizational contexts. In particular, the general approach to understanding organizational culture in partnership work is too often overly simplistic and fails to drill down into the specific behaviors, beliefs, and contextual factors that shape cultural dynamics in schools and universities.

Thus, the field needs a new approach to studying education partnerships that opens the black box of partnerships and examines how individual, cultural, and organizational factors influence partnership operations. Accordingly, our approach is built on the following elements.

### Individual Mental Models

First, we focus on the individual psychology of partnership participants—the teachers, faculty, staff, and administrators who make decisions, plan programs, and teach lessons in classrooms. Each of these actors has particular ways of interpreting the world and new information, called "mental models." As people interact with the world and develop habits and memories of particular routines, they encode this information into their long-term memories, such that new information is then interpreted in light of the mental models that already exist. Management scholars such as Senge (1994) suggest that mental models are critically important in understanding people's behaviors and decisions in organizations, because they constitute the lens through which people understand the world.

## Cultural Dynamics Within Complex Organizations

Mental models do not operate in a vacuum, as if our minds were immune from the surrounding social and organizational environment. Advances in cognitive psychology show that cognition is enabled and constrained by particular situations, and thus our mental models are deeply embedded within the specific organizational and sociocultural environments in which we live and work. This makes sense when you consider, for example, that a mental model for how to teach long division is acquired in a very particular organizational context (e.g., the university department in which an elementary or secondary teacher took math courses). Researchers have long focused on the role of culture in shaping individual-level cognition and on how the ingrained beliefs, practices, and organizations that structure our lives foster each person's unique ways of viewing the world and solving problems (e.g., Lave, 1988). Since the cultural differences among K–12 schools and IHEs, and among different disciplines, are often cited as critical stumbling blocks for partnerships, we pay close attention to how the cultural dynamics within educational organizations influence partnerships. Most of us intuitively recognize that schools and IHEs have a cultural component, usually thought of as the "way things are done around here," as well as particular symbols or rituals unique to a given site. However, instead of viewing organizational culture as simply the beliefs and values of a group (i.e., the ideational component of culture), we adopt a more traditional and anthropological view of culture as comprising structural, ideational, and behavioral components.

In addition, culture is too often thought of as something that can be easily created or changed in schools or IHEs. Such a view leads to strategies akin to those adopted in the Internet bubble years by some Silicon Valley companies, which installed Ping-Pong tables in staff lounges to "create a culture of creativity." Instead, as Fried and Hansson (2010) argue, "culture happens," and it is "the by-product of consistent behavior" within very specific environments (p. 249). Thus, we argue for a more multifaceted view of culture that takes into account not only the beliefs and values of a group but also the organizational milieu in which they are embedded. In particular, we focus on four interrelated aspects of organizational life—cultural models, structure and technologies, relationships, and routines and practices—that together constitute the cultural dynamics of a K–12 school or IHE (see Figure 1).

*Cultural models.* A cultural model is a deeply held belief or interpretation of the world that is shared among members of a particular group. For instance, some faculty in a math department may have a mental model that the best way for undergraduate students to learn is to memorize theorems and practice computational problems, whereas other faculty may have a model that students should focus instead on a deep conceptual understanding of the material. A mental model that is largely shared among group members is called a cultural model. Note that a group's cultural models might or might not align with those of larger organizational entities of which the group is a

## FIGURE 1
**Component parts of cultural dynamics within education organizations**

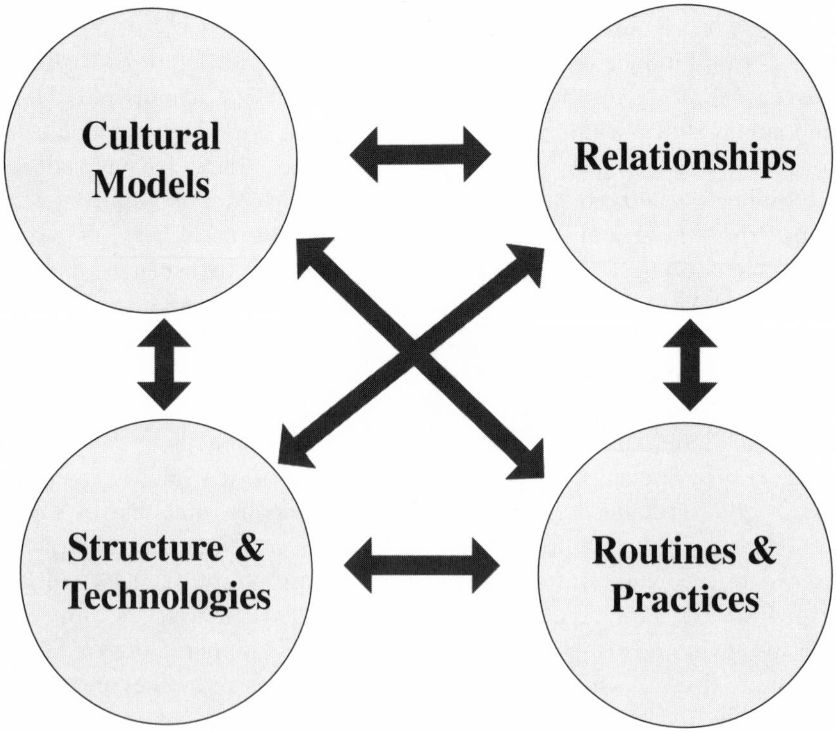

part: our example math department has two cultural models for teaching. In this way, cultural model theory accounts for the presence of subcultures, which, as we all know, exist in any school or university. By contrast, a generalized statement about an organization's "culture" does not account for the variety of beliefs and practices within an organization.

*Relationships.* A relationship is a key aspect of cultural life that ties an individual to other people, groups, and organizations. Relationships in organizations provide the opportunity for beliefs and knowledge to become shared among groups of people, as well as for camaraderie—or enmity—to develop over time. Thus, ongoing relationships within a K–12 school or IHE constitute one of the main conduits through which cultural models are shared and transferred and the venue for a shared sense of identity to develop.

*Structure and technologies.* Anthropologists have long focused on the structural features of a society as a critical aspect of a group's culture. How a group's social hierarchy is structured, the technology it uses, and the organization of its economy are but a few of the structural components of a group that constitute the milieu in which people live and work and develop cultural models about various topics. In education, the programs, policies, and hierarchy of a school or university can be considered part of the organizational structure. These structural features establish the parameters of what behaviors are possible, permissible, and rewarded. For instance, tenure and promotion policies establish the criteria by which individual teachers and faculty will be judged and have the effect of delimiting the range of behaviors in which individuals are likely to engage. In this way, an organization's structure and technologies form an important part of the cultural dynamics of K–12 schools and IHEs.

*Routines and practices.* Individuals and groups in organizations also engage in routines: regular, patterned behaviors that eventually become habitual. For example, a high school science department may have weekly meetings to discuss issues ranging from the curriculum to student management issues. These routines give meaning and identity to people's roles within an organization, such that the roles (e.g., second-grade teacher, physics department faculty member) become inextricably linked with particular routines. Thus, the structure of an organization creates some opportunities (and constrains others) for certain routines and practices, which in turn contribute to the development of a group's cultural models.

## Cultural Dynamics and Affinity Groups

When these four features of cultural dynamics come together, you often find a particular group of individuals who occupy a similar niche in an organization, have ongoing relationships, share similar beliefs and knowledge, and engage in similar routines. These groups typically exhibit close ties and a shared sense of identity that is more pronounced and influential than the ties and identity wrought because of people simply being members of the same K–12 school or IHE. For instance, within a typical high school, you may find that the teachers and staff in the science department hold similar beliefs, are subject to the same procedures and policies, and engage in tasks in ways that are distinct from other departments. Jim Gee (2007), an education researcher, uses the term, "affinity groups," for groups of people who share a particular craft or set of interests (p. 27). In an affinity group, members develop a unique language, share social and behavioral norms, and socialize new members to act in accordance with the group's ethos. Understanding the idiosyncratic aspects of affinity groups within home organizations is crucial to understanding how individuals and groups will function in a partnership. The cultural models, relationships, structure and technologies, and routines and practices that distinguish affinity groups from one another (e.g., administrators, physics university faculty, and a high school science department) constitute a core aspect of the "preexisting conditions" that members of each partner organization will carry into the partnership realm.

> Understanding the idiosyncratic aspects of affinity groups within home organizations is important to understanding how individuals and groups will function in a partnership.

## Fostering Learning and New Cultural Dynamics in the 3rd Space

Finally, our approach relies heavily on the concept of the partnership realm as a "3rd space," by which we mean an entirely new arena for activity in which competing interests, perspectives, and opinions play out as different organizations come together and working groups form and begin operating. The concept of the 3rd space was first introduced to describe classroom learning communities where students and teachers from different backgrounds and perspectives came together to transform conflict into zones of collaboration and learning. The 3rd-space concept enables us to view each partnership working group as an emerging technical and sociocultural entity distinct from those within the partnership's home organizations. Within the 3rd space of a specific working group, individuals from the different home organizations navigate their different preexisting cultural dynamics as they develop the policies and repertoires of practice appropriate for the new partnership (see Figure 2).

Thinking of partnership work as occurring in a 3rd space sheds light on the cultural dynamics of cross-organizational work. It helps us see partnerships as emergent and multivocal in nature, as organizations that evolve over time as group members negotiate and begin to use new shared meanings. Researchers who study interorganizational relations also emphasize the unpredictable nature of collaborative work and the fact that the absence of familiar organizational structures and routines creates a working environment that is characterized by change. The unpredictable nature of the 3rd space holds both challenges and promises. It is challenging to create an entirely new organization comprising people from diverse backgrounds, often with demanding timelines and limited resources. At the same time, creating new organizational structures, relationships, and practices provides the opportunity for new ways of thinking and acting to emerge. Over time, if a group's members work well together and begin to develop a shared sense of identity and language, new cultural models may also emerge. Such creation of new cultural dynamics is powerful and transformative. The 3rd space has strong potential as a learning environment because it invites, indeed requires, creativity and the application of diverse forms of knowledge to new problems. Thus, the routine expertise you have developed in your home organization may or may not be well suited to your partnership tasks, since these represent a new set of problems and situations. Instead, you likely will need to adapt your expertise and knowledge to these new tasks, an approach that is a cornerstone of innovation and creativity.

We use the 3rd space as a central metaphor in this book because it enables teachers, administrators, and policy makers to remember that to use partnerships as a strategy for addressing pressing educational challenges requires deft negotiation of differences in an uncertain and ever-changing environment. Our approach is informed by our training as anthropologists and the conviction that anthropology can help address the challenges facing partnerships. As Clyde Kluckhohn (1949) famously said, "Anthropology provides a scientific basis for dealing with the crucial dilemma of the world today: how can peoples of different appearance, mutually unintelligible languages, and dissimilar ways of life get along peaceably together?" (p. 1). Because many partnerships fail to reconcile these differences, we offer an

# FIGURE 2

## Components of partnership formation in the 3rd space

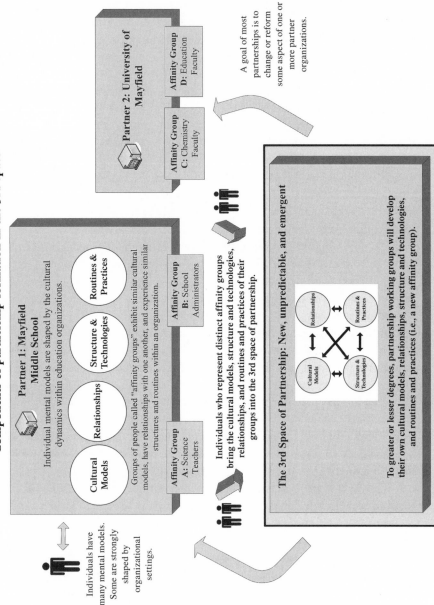

approach to improve practitioners' understanding of how these differences influence partnerships and how to manage these differences.

## The Five Principles of Partnership

Here is an overview of the five underlying principles that constitute the basic message of the book.

1. Think of organizations and partnerships in multifaceted terms.

   The organizations within partnerships, and partnerships themselves, should be understood not as monolithic wholes, but as comprising subgroups that differ in ways that may matter to the success of a partnership. Instead of thinking of a school or an IHE as a singular entity (e.g., Mayfair University or Mayfair Middle School), focus on the specific departments or administrative units that will be participating in the partnership (e.g., the Mayfair University Chemistry Department, or the Mayfair Middle School Science Department). In addition, try to avoid thinking of these organizations and groups in terms of a particular "type" or "culture." Instead, focus on the specific structure and technologies, cultural models, relationships, and routines and practices that actually characterize organizational life for these groups. If you develop the habit of viewing the organizations involved in your partnership in this way, you will gain a more adequate understanding of how and why people do what they do, and will increase opportunities for crafting 3rd-space working environments that foster new ways of thinking and acting.

2. Plan and get acquainted.

   The literature is in agreement that partnerships should begin with a careful planning stage, where all potential partners meet and get acquainted with one another and clearly discuss the proposed work. This involves not only getting to know the key personalities in the other organizations and developing a sense of familiarity and collegiality, but also learning the basics about how their organizations operate. This is important because it is easy to assume that the way business is done in other groups is the same as in your own, but this is rarely the case. For instance, physics departments at two different IHEs may have completely different governance procedures, interactions with the K–12 sector, ideas about how to best improve undergraduate instruction, and so on. But before you begin getting acquainted with potential partners, you need to diagnose those attributes of your own organization that are relevant to establishing a partnership—*know thyself.* This is necessary because each partnering organization must surface for itself, as well as for the others, its often tacit views about how to solve problems. Each group must also identify how these views relate to the proposed partnership goals and objectives, and ideas about administration and governance. In addition, if your organization is quite large, it is important to ensure that relevant groups or factions within it agree on these matters before engaging in the larger partnership. So the first step is to hold internal discussions about the proposed work and its implications for your organization.

We then recommend that you discuss these issues openly in pre-partnership planning meetings that bring representatives from different organizations together. This is a good way to start things off on an informed and, we hope, positive footing. At these meetings, you need to discuss critical issues, such as goals and objectives for the partnership, the nature of the problem at hand, how much autonomy your organization will need to maintain, cultural tensions, and so on. Based on the results of this meeting, you can decide whether moving forward is in the best interests of all parties. If so, this may result in a proposal being developed for a competitive grant program, or a memorandum of understanding to create a partnership on the spot. The core idea proposed here is that before taking these steps, you need to hold planning meetings in which all parties come to an initial understanding of one another, the nature of the work being proposed, and the local conditions and contingencies in which the work will be grounded.

3. Engage in a careful design process.

Once you have agreed to proceed, it is time to begin designing the organizational structure for the partnership. Because newly initiated partnerships lack structure and procedures, starting them is akin to creating entirely new organizations: organizational hierarchies, policies and procedures governing task delegation and performance accountability, and other critical features of functioning organizations all must be established. But forming a partnership is further complicated by the fact that the preexisting needs and constraints of multiple organizations need to be considered when crafting the partnership's structures and procedures. Because the organizational structure of a partnership will guide decision making, task implementation, and administration, if these features are at odds with the existing cultural dynamics of the partner organizations, a smoothly operating partnership is unlikely. Thus, choosing the organizational structure and designing its procedures are among the most important activities in the 3rd space of partnership, and these are not simple tasks.

Unfortunately, it is this stage that many administrators cite as their worst experience with collaboration. If you and your partners fail at this early point to demarcate boundaries and create effective structures and procedures, you likely will exacerbate, rather than address, the inherent tensions in partnership work (Thomson & Perry, 2006). To avoid this negative experience and increase your chances of ultimate success, take the time at the beginning to design organizational structures and administrative procedures that fit the nature of your goals and objectives (e.g., technical or adaptive problems), the relevant "inherited" features of the partner organizations, and other aspects of your partnership. Include partnership evaluation—an often overlooked feature—in your design work. Evaluation findings will help provide you and other leaders with accurate and actionable information to navigate the complexities of partnership cultural dynamics and operations. Moreover, because leaders need to identify and respond to problems in real time, not after the fact, we and other partnership researchers encourage practitioners to use formative evaluation. It is in this design stage where a one-size-fits-all model is particularly inappropriate. It would be a mistake to adopt a partnership structure off the shelf. Carefully identify local conditions, and use the information gleaned in the pre-partnership planning meeting to determine the most appropriate organization for your particular situation.

---

You must carefully diagnose the differences among the organizations in your partnership and then craft structures and procedures that encourage meaningful interactions across structural and cultural boundaries.

4. Cultivate personnel who are boundary crossers.

   Once the partnership is designed, successful implementation depends on the presence of staff and leaders who are both flexible and able to cross organizational and cultural boundaries. Indeed, the driving assumption behind our approach to management in the 3rd space of partnership is captured by Barbara Gray's (1989) description of collaboration as the "constructive management of differences" (p. 1). Given the unpredictable nature of partnerships—where events and conditions change all the time—your personnel will need to contend with unpredictable challenges, differences of opinion among the participants, and the likely need to adapt to changing circumstances. At all organizational levels, these individuals will need to contend with the cultural and organizational boundaries that separate different organizations, disciplines, and stakeholders. These boundaries may result in misinterpretations of events or documents, or even outright conflict. Effective boundary crossers can anticipate and mitigate these tensions, largely because they tend to be good listeners, can empathize, take careful notice of others' views and tacit assumptions, and can find common ground among different parties. They should also be savvy at dealing with the inevitable conflicts that will emerge, whether minor disagreements over the naming of a workshop or major disputes over resources or leadership. Therefore, people who can effectively span these boundaries are critical.

5. Take advantage of the opportunity to foster new cultural dynamics.

   Recall that the deeply held values and beliefs of a group, or their cultural models, are linked to specific structural features of an organization, relationships, and practices. This means that in the 3rd space of partnership work, you have the opportunity to create task environments that will foster new structures, relationships, and practices that in turn may generate new ways of thinking. For example, bringing IHE and K–12 faculty to a common table to develop a new science curriculum will require holding meetings, establishing policies and procedures for communication, and delegating tasks to individuals or groups. If each of these groups is asked to participate solely as an expert of its own domain (e.g., IHE faculty as content experts, K–12 faculty as pedagogy experts), new cultural dynamics are unlikely to emerge. In contrast, if these groups are forced to work collaboratively on a common task, and are engaged as both experts and learners, then the likelihood of new cultural dynamics increases. The 3rd space of partnership offers a wonderful opportunity to create a new working environment. It is up to you to craft it so that it will encourage new ways of thinking and acting.

It is also important to recognize the opportunity that conflict presents in partnership work. The outcomes of conflict are not necessarily negative; in fact, conflict and cognitive dissonance are sometimes necessary to get groups to explore new ideas and possibilities. By quickly diagnosing and collectively solving problems, you can renew and strengthen the trust and social cohesion among partners. On the other hand, by ignoring or dealing ineffectively with conflict, you likely will undermine the trust and collective identity of a partnership. Remember that the goal of creating a 3rd space of partnership is not to create a single way of doing things, or a "common culture," but to harness different views and areas of expertise in a productive manner.

## How to Use This Book

How should you use this book? We wrote this book primarily for K–12 and IHE practitioners who either are considering whether to engage in partnership work or are actively engaged in designing and managing a partnership. In either case, although you may find it valuable to peruse the book's chapters at random, honing in on issues that interest you the most, we designed the book to be read from start to finish. This is because partnerships should be carefully planned and then designed based on key principles that need to be discussed at the very early stages. If these topics are ignored, then the tasks and operational structures you establish may operate on very shaky ground. In fact, we suggest you hold a series of pre-partnership meetings during which you try to identify likely opportunities and sources of conflict, pay attention to your hunches, and assess whether to pursue a partnership at all (see Figure 3).

This approach is based, in part, on Tuckman and Jensen's (1977) model of group development, in which groups go through five distinct phases to foster growth, effective problem solving, and eventual success:

- forming (individuals meet and get to know one another);
- storming (different ideas are considered and debated);

# FIGURE 3

## How to use this book to plan, implement, and monitor your partnership

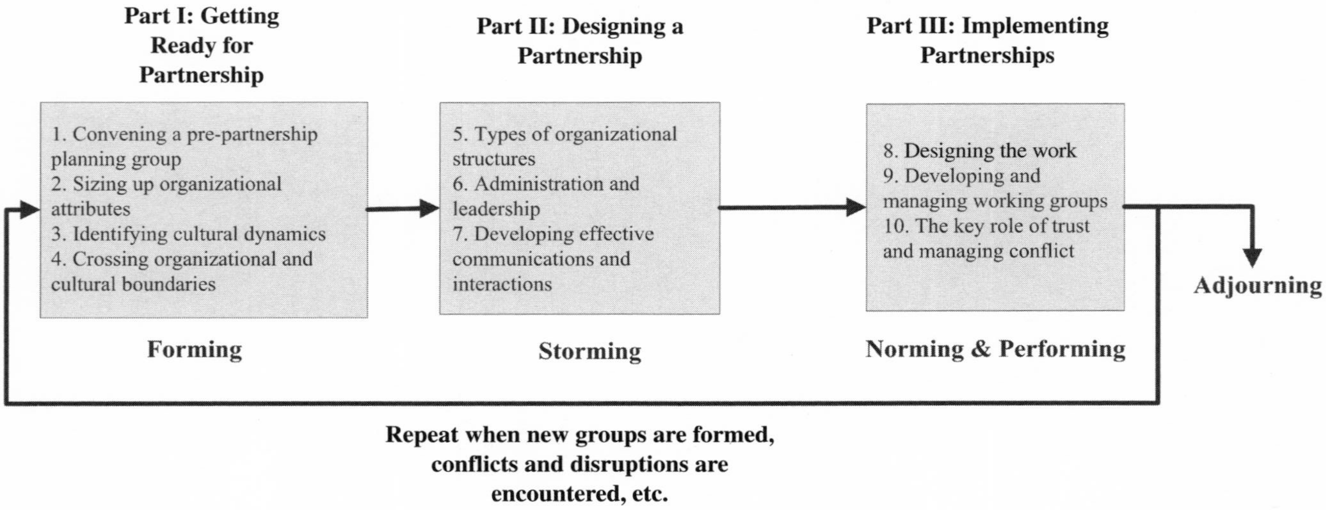

| Part I: Getting Ready for Partnership | Part II: Designing a Partnership | Part III: Implementing Partnerships |
|---|---|---|
| 1. Convening a pre-partnership planning group<br>2. Sizing up organizational attributes<br>3. Identifying cultural dynamics<br>4. Crossing organizational and cultural boundaries | 5. Types of organizational structures<br>6. Administration and leadership<br>7. Developing effective communications and interactions | 8. Designing the work<br>9. Developing and managing working groups<br>10. The key role of trust and managing conflict |
| Forming | Storming | Norming & Performing |

Adjourning

Repeat when new groups are formed, conflicts and disruptions are encountered, etc.

- norming (group members adjust behavior and agree on rules and procedures);
- performing (group members become interdependent and the group functions well); and
- adjourning (the group's activities conclude).

Use the principles introduced in part one to begin a conversation about partnering and to enter into the forming stage prepared to identify the kinds of things that you and your partners must learn about one another. Then, it is time for the diverse participants to begin storming, as you discuss your separate and potentially shared goals and motivations, the desired degree of interdependence, cultural tensions that likely will surface, and whether you have leaders who can effectively cross the organizational and cultural boundaries that characterize partnership work. By addressing these topics, you are more likely to diagnose, in broad terms, what is and is not possible and desirable.

In part two we present key steps in designing a partnership. This is when groups begin the norming phase. These steps include determining the appropriate partnership structure, administration and governance procedures, and communication systems. For instance, we suggest that an effective system for monitoring and assessing problems and conflict should be established to provide leaders with information needed to make needed midcourse corrections. Finally, in part three we discuss some of the most important aspects of partnership implementation and management. We emphasize that during this stage of group performing, circumstances will likely change, and even the best-laid plans may require reassessment or retooling. However, if handled with adaptive expertise, such unpredictability and volatility can become a learning opportunity, which makes persevering in the face of adversity a potentially valuable decision. At this stage a working group will continue its operations in a smooth fashion, complete its work, and adjourn, or it will evolve into a new entity. In the likelihood that a group encounters challenges or is dramatically changed, we recommend revisiting the steps in parts one and two.

Finally, we wish to emphasize that this is not a how-to book for establishing, implementing, and managing every conceivable type of partnership, much less the three types on which we focus. How partnerships are established, designed, and led differs considerably, depending on their type, purpose, and expected outcomes. Instead, we offer a way to think about partnership work that should allow you to clarify your own partnership's type, purpose, and outcomes and help you to decide which facets of design and management need to be considered. Again, there is no one-size-fits-all model for education partnership, but there are guidelines and key points that everyone would benefit from by considering in depth.

## Bibliographic Note

A bibliographic note at the end of each chapter includes citations to books and articles on which we have drawn in our analysis (see References, pages 197–203, for complete information). In this note, we emphasize that we did not conduct exhaustive reviews of the literature on partnership and collaboration in every possible field—such a task is beyond the purview of this book.

For a review of the education partnership literature through the late 1980s, see Richard Clark's chapter in Sirotnik and Goodlad (1988); for a more recent analysis, see Waschak and Kingsley (2006). The latter article also provides an overview of different methods and conceptual frameworks used to analyze and evaluate partnerships. For a review of the rationale behind education partnerships, see Hodgkinson (1999). For a sampling of the extensive literature on education partnerships, see Amey, Eddy, and Ozaki (2007); R. W. Clark (1999b); Houck, Cohn, and Cohn (2004); Johnston (1997); Mitchell (2002); Ravid and Handler (2001); and Sirotnik and Goodlad (1988). Two books stand out for their innovative theoretical approach to partnerships: Borthwick (2001) draws on the French sociologist Pierre Bourdieu's ideas of habitus to explore how individual dispositions are shaped by the cultural environment and in turn shape partnership work, and Tsui, Edwards, and Lopez-Real (2009) employ situated-cognition theory to examine how the task environment enables and constrains individual and group interactions and learning throughout the course of a partnership.

Although the literature on partnership and collaboration in organization and administrative science is too voluminous to summarize adequately here, we mention a few of the works we consider most useful. We found excellent insights in Barbara Gray's 1989 analysis of collaborative work, Ring and Van de Ven's 1994 analysis of interorganizational relations, and Thomson and Perry's 2006 examination of the internal mechanisms of interorganizational relations. Similarly, there is extensive literature on creativity and innovation in these fields. For a good discussion, see March's 1991 seminal work on exploration and exploitation, and see Heifitz (1994) for a discussion of technical and adaptive challenges. For a discussion on the idea of the 3rd space in education, see Gutierrez, Baquedano-Lopez, and Tejada (1999), and see Tsui and Law (2007) as it pertains specifically to education partnerships.

Our conceptual framework is influenced by Halverson's 2003 discussion of systems of practice in schools and by work on situated cognition that brings together psychological, cultural, and organizational factors to understand human behavior. For a discussion of this latter area, see Brown, Collins, and Duguid (1989); Greeno (1998); and Lave (1988). We also draw on Jim Gee's 2007 work for the idea of affinity groups, which is preferable to the more widely used "communities of practice" idea that conveys a certain romanticism regarding group identity and operations. See Spillane, Reiser, and Reimer (2002) for an excellent review of the literature on school reform from this perspective, and Kezar and Eckel (2002) and Tierney (2008) for an analysis of organizational culture and its relationship to change strategies. See Austin (1996) for an introduction to cultural factors at the institutional and departmental level in IHEs and their relationship to teaching.

For a thorough review of culture theory as it is used in organizational analysis, see Martin (2002), and for a quick primer on controversies regarding the idea of culture in anthropology, see Clifford and Marcus (1986). Our work is largely based in the anthropological subfield of cognitive anthropology; for good analyses of this field, see D'Andrade (1995) and Strauss and Quinn (1997). The idea of cultural models is based on the work of cognitive anthropologists, but also see Gee (2007) for a superb analysis of how these models function in relation to learning. For an excellent discussion of ethnography and how to adopt an anthropological view when faced with new situations or study populations, see Agar (1996). Finally, for more information about the methods used in our analysis, see Yin (2003) for a discussion about the case-study method and Miles and Huberman (1994) for a step-by-step description of causal network analysis.

# PART ONE

## GETTING READY FOR PARTNERSHIP

If I had to do the partnership over, I would have waited and spent 3 to 5 months up front getting to know the partners better, and then started working together rather than trying to hit the ground running from day one.

(University administrator)

Part one focuses on how to begin a conversation about partnering and enter the forming and storming stages of group development. We outline six guidelines for conducting pre-partnership planning meetings in chapter 1. Here we also explain why pre-partnership planning, which too often is given short shrift, is one of the most important steps for successful partnerships. This discussion is followed by three chapters that delve into greater detail on the types of things you should be considering at this early stage of partnership. In chapter 2, we discuss sizing up organizational aspirations and attributes, chapter 3 focuses on identifying cultural dynamics, and chapter 4 includes a discussion of crossing organizational and cultural boundaries.

# I

# SHALL WE DANCE?

When the UDEP partnership leaders received word that their proposal had been funded, they hurriedly convened a planning session at a hub airport. More than 10 leaders from four cities flew in and met in an airport conference room. After consulting the funding agency's guidelines, they began hammering out details about the partnership goals and producing benchmarks, timelines, and a strategies. The group held several more meetings and exchanged hundreds of e-mails and phone calls before finally submitting a detailed strategic plan to the funding organization. This plan detailed the various goals of the partnership and how different organizations were to work collaboratively to improve math and science instruction in large, urban K–12 districts. The group chose a collaborative partnership structure, in which decisions would be made by a senior leadership group comprising representatives from K–12 and IHE partner organizations.

The management system that emerged from this planning period did not survive, however. Different members of the senior leadership group brought ideas about partnership roles, responsibilities, and decision-making arrangements from their home organizations. Within months it became clear that the cross-organizational leadership group that was supposed to be the core of a collaborative enterprise was divided by competing interests and conflicting leadership styles. There was no agreed-on process for managing this situation, because policies for communication, power sharing, and decision making were either unstated or ineffective. The senior leadership group functioned ineffectively for about 18 months, and this situation was exacerbated by the introduction of a new IHE into the partnership. As the partnership moved into its third year, it was tacitly understood that leadership decisions were being made by different groups, reflecting suballiances among the partner institutions. These groups sometimes worked at cross-purposes, and eventually the partnership was dissolved. What went wrong?

---

**Partnership Action Point:** Partners should hold meetings in which they discuss the nature of the problem to be addressed, goals of the partnership, the specific objectives and tasks to achieve those goals, and other key features of partnership work *prior to* actually engaging in a partnership.

---

While partnership has the potential to effect positive change in the lives of the partners' students, teachers, faculty, administrators, and organizations as a whole, there will be many roadblocks in the road to success. Given the inevitable challenges, it makes sense to plot a course carefully, consider all options, and take care to know who it is you're getting involved with. In fact, funders increasingly are requiring evidence of the involvement and commitment of partner organizations in a strategic planning process before approving an award or a grant. Ideally, the UDEP partners would have engaged in a deliberate process of getting acquainted with one another over the course of weeks or months, as several UDEP participants expressed in hindsight. They made ample recommendations on this point, including, "You should know what you're getting into" and "Lots of up-front work needs to be done so leaders understand each other's perspectives and needs." However, like most organizations considering partnerships, UDEP participants did not have the luxury of several months during which to scrutinize potential partners and assess compatibility. Their partnership was forged in the fire of a grant opportunity announced just months before the proposal deadline. Each partner organization only had time to make a quick appraisal of one another's track records and professional reputations.

In the UDEP grant proposal, a handful of leaders, primarily from two IHEs, designed a complex collaboration whose goal was to transform teaching math and science to children in large, urban school districts. The main preexisting connection among the partners was the professional relationship of two leaders who had known of each other for years but had never worked closely together. This mutual lack of knowledge had deleterious effects, in no small part because there was no foundation of trust or familiarity upon which to base a collective vision and identity (Gray, 1989). In addition, a new IHE partner came into the project and ended up working far more closely with one original partner than the other, thus exacerbating an already tenuous working relationship. The entry of a new partner also meant that any shared sense of vision or trust among the original partners would need to be re-created to include all of the partner organizations, but this ultimately did not take place. Perhaps most deleterious was the fact that the leaders did not explicitly identify the senior leadership group's responsibilities or its meeting and decision-making processes. The leaders did not explicitly attend to decisions about the partnership's overall organizational structure, the roles and responsibilities of the senior leaders, who would make which types of decisions, and how these decisions would be made.

These features of partnership should not be left unexplored or implicit but should be clearly discussed as part of a deliberative planning process. Such a process identifies and implements the most appropriate organizational structure and procedure for each unique situation and sets in motion the development of professional relationships. By exploring crucial topics up front, potential partners can identify areas of congruence and overlap that may indicate the potential for effective collaboration. This information-sharing process also deepens partners' understanding of the problems they are jointly seeking to address. It also may uncover areas of disagreement or discord that signal a need to slow down, talk things over, and begin exploring a way to forge some sort of consensus. Because the 3rd space of partnership is so unpredictable, it is also desirable to take this additional time up front to get to know your partners so you can begin your journey with at least some sense of familiarity, trust, and foresight about the road ahead.

## Convening a Pre-Partnership Planning Group

How do you obtain all this valuable information about an organization's procedures, a group's cultural models and routines, and leaders' personalities? We recommend paying close attention to the forming stage of group development. When faced with new interagency collaborations or disruptive events such as acquisitions or changing economic conditions, companies hire outside firms to conduct organizational audits. The goal of such audits is to help organizations better understand their internal procedures, increase efficiencies, and manage the risks associated with working with different organizations to "effectively manage risk across organizational boundaries" (Deloitte & Touche, 2009). Based on these audits' findings, companies then

decide whether to proceed with a partnership, and if they do decide to proceed, to plan their collaboration or merger strategically. (Indeed, several of
the people we interviewed stated that if an organizational audit had been
conducted the UDEP partners would have decided against proceeding.) Yet,
in education, few companies provide these services, so practitioners are generally left to their own devices.

In this section we present a cost-effective and efficient way to initiate
conversations about organizational characteristics and cultural dynamics.
Based on our experience observing ways these conversations can be successfully initiated and conducted in other multiagency collaborations, we suggest
holding two or three meetings for representatives of each potential partner
organization. These meetings provide a forum for bringing to the surface
and honestly appraising relevant organizational, cultural, and individual
characteristics. This approach is also based on Jim Collins's idea of a "council," where representatives from stakeholder groups within a company meet
regularly to "gain understanding about important issues facing the organization" (Collins, 2001, p. 115). This council is charged to vigorously debate the
goals and objectives of a company in a spirit of camaraderie and focus only
on the "brutal facts." In a partnership setting, this group, which we call the
pre-partnership planning group, serves as a venue where representatives can
report on the key characteristics of their school, district, department, or
university. With this information clarified, the planning council can then
collectively assess the prospects for continuing the partnership effort and
identify any potential trouble spots.

### Step 1: Select Participants for the Planning Group

The first step of a partnership is selecting the individuals, groups, and organizations with which you would like to partner. You might have prior professional contacts who may either become partners or suggest suitable
individuals or organizations with which to collaborate. Or the range of possible partners may be limited by funders' or policy makers' stipulations. For
example, if you plan to apply for a grant that requires your K–12 school to
partner with a local IHE (as was the case with the aforementioned Georgia
Early College Initiative), you probably will seek possible partners from the
local pool of K–12 schools or IHEs. In other cases, a local or regional educational crisis may bring various leaders together to discuss how to deal with
the situation. In the early 1990s, Long Beach, California, was experiencing a
rise in gang violence, unemployment, and perilously low student test scores.
In response, leaders from the Long Beach Unified School District, Long

Beach City College, and California State University at Long Beach formed a partnership whose goal was to prepare students for college without the need for remedial education.

Once you've identified potential partners, you need to identify which individuals should participate in the planning group. Since each partnership will be formed under unique local conditions, we do not offer suggestions for how to approach individuals from K–12 schools or IHEs to begin the planning process; instead, we focus on what to discuss once you have a group of potential partners around the table. This is a critical step. Even if you feel there is not enough time or funding to engage in this process, we strongly urge you to hold at least one meeting to ascertain whether a partnership is actually in the best interests of everyone involved.

In addition to representatives from each potential partner organization, you should include a program evaluator from the very start if possible, for two reasons. First, an experienced evaluator can help you identify whether the goals and objectives for the proposed effort are measurable and can point you to relevant sources of data pertaining to the proposed work. Second, the evaluator will be able to identify ways a formative evaluation could be useful. If you are still in the initial planning stages and do not have an evaluator, it is not too late to add one. When inviting people to these planning meetings, try to include individuals who (1) not only represent all of the potential partner organizations but also have close ties with the work units (e.g., a high school science department) that will be directly involved in the partnership work, (2) are known for their tendency to interact respectfully with other people and their capacity to work according to a group's ground rules, and (3) have sufficient time to participate regularly for the expected duration of the partnership.

Regarding the first criterion—selecting people who adequately represent each organization—first ask which organizational units need to be represented to develop the programs and manage partnership procedures, and then decide whether one person can play this role or if several will be needed. Barbara Intriligator (1992) stresses the importance of engaging a high-level administrator (a superintendent or dean) in the early planning process to convey to participants the importance of the partnership. If this administrator does not have much local experience, you should consider selecting one or more people who work at middle management (unit leaders) and one or more from the local level (such as a teacher or faculty member). Such people can bring knowledge about how to design the work in ways that align well with local situations, ways of viewing the problem at hand (i.e., local cultural models), and particular needs related to the work (e.g., time, materials). In addition to bringing a clear understanding of the possible challenges of implementation, middle- and ground-level workers can help identify and clarify some of the cultural differences among the partner organizations. By including them, you also may increase partnership buy-in from diverse groups at the middle and ground levels. Ideally, you also will include individuals who represent diverse opinions within the organization. The challenge is to include people who can adequately represent as many of the relevant organizational standpoints as possible while keeping the size of the planning group small enough to function effectively.

It is at least as important to meet the second criterion as it is the first. Seely Brown and Duguid (2002) emphasize the importance of ensuring that all participants have the capacity to treat one another with mutual respect while also debating and disagreeing with one another. As we have noted, the council participants' main initial tasks are to surface preexisting ideas and assumptions that each brings about key topics (such as how to collaborate with others or how best to solve the problem under consideration), gain at least some understanding of other participants, identify the degree to which they have common ground, and then decide whether the differences can be turned to advantage or will lead to an impasse. To undertake such emotionally and socially challenging work in an atmosphere that is anything but respectful is not feasible.

### Step 2: Select an Objective and Skilled Facilitator

Your planning group meetings should be managed by an objective and skilled person who can facilitate efficient and effective interactions among a wide variety of people, many of whom represent different organizations and experiences. Although it is tempting to ignore the step of choosing a facilitator, the cost of doing so is likely to be high. If you are among the leaders who initially seek to form a partnership planning group, find a third-party meeting facilitator with a reputation for helping all participants to feel safe to voice their opinions and ideas. Then invite your potential partners to either agree to this person or suggest an equally or better-qualified facilitator. One of the facilitator's charges should be to ensure that meetings run smoothly. This includes setting clear agendas that result in specific courses of action as opposed to a simple list of topics to be discussed. Facilitators should also be able to keep participants on task and to work toward creating an atmosphere in which all participants feel comfortable expressing their points of view. This can be done by ensuring that individuals with high status or power do not dominate the discussion, and that participants do not interrupt one another or otherwise demonstrate a lack of regard for one another. To manage meetings in such a manner requires a strong hand, and if you cannot secure the services of such a facilitator, at the very least, tap one of the potential leaders of the group to act as a facilitator for the planning group meetings. The last thing you want at this critical forming stage is for participants' time and energy to be wasted in unstructured meetings.

### Step 3: Come to the Meetings Prepared

Participants should come to the meetings prepared to participate actively. This involves canvassing the participants for the key topics that need to be discussed, which can then be circulated in advance so that each participant can consider ahead of time his or her stance on each item (see Table 1). In addition, someone will have to be responsible for asking other participants within their own organizations for this information, or alternatively, an individual can collect the information. Ideally, meetings should be held within your organization before the planning group meetings, to help participants bring subconscious cultural models to a conscious level. That is, a certain amount of reflection is required to identify your own mental and cultural models before you can bring them to a planning council.

### TABLE 1
**Key topics to discuss at your pre-partnership planning meeting**

| *From part one* | *From part two* | *From part three* |
|---|---|---|
| Goals or vision for the effort | Types of partnership | Partnership tasks (i.e., how related to stakeholders) |
| Specific objectives to achieve goals (i.e., the actual work) | Governance and decision making | Working group formation and management |
| Nature of the problem (i.e., technical or adaptive) | Fiscal management | The role of trust |
| Motivations for participation | Program evaluation | Conflict resolution |
| Organizational capacity/ resources | Communications technology and procedures | |
| Degree of desired interdependence | | |
| Cultural dynamics related to the work | | |

Several of the topics to discuss are covered in detail in the rest of part one; they include goals and objectives, motivations, organizational capacity, interdependence, cultural models, and boundary crossing. Below are guidelines for considering these topics at your pre-partnership planning meetings.

### *Identify Your Goals and Objectives and Assess Whether These Warrant a Partnership*

To ensure that all members of your partnership understand the goals and objectives, strive from the very beginning to define them clearly and to everyone's satisfaction. Failure to do this leads to the all too common situation in which partners have different views of the goals and objectives. Check frequently with participants to ensure that the inevitable variations in how people interpret the goals and objectives do not result in a veneer of common understanding covering seriously different views of the work.

### *State Your Real Motivations*

Although it may seem impolitic to ask potential partners to articulate their real motivations, it is important to ensure that a partnership works to advance everyone's interests. First consider your own individual and organizational motivations for becoming involved in the partnership—such reflection is essential because motivations may be largely tacit and unarticulated. Such an exercise should be informative on an internal basis, and ideally you will share relevant aspects of these motivations with the larger group. Although it is natural to keep your motivations private, for the well-being of your own organization and the potential partnership, it is important to communicate honestly some aspect of your true motivations.

### *Identify Organizational Capacity to Participate*

Think of the planning group meetings as a kind of mutual job interview: you need to know before you "hire" one another what types of resources each of you can potentially contribute and whether these resources are actually available. Encourage participants to be as frank and specific as possible about their expertise, the amount of leadership and staff time they can release to the entire partnership, the size and nature of the professional networks they can activate on behalf of the partnership, and the material resources— including space, communications equipment, and back-office support—they can offer.

*Assess Motivations and Organizational Need for Autonomy Against the*
*Level of Interdependence Required to Achieve the Goals*

By definition, a partnership begins as a loosely coupled system, and leaders must begin assessing how much interdependence will be needed to achieve the partnership's goals. This decision will be driven by the nature of the goals, whether specific partners are viewed as having—and whether they actually have—the resources needed to achieve the goals, and the degree to which tightly coupled processes and structures are required to achieve those goals. For instance, a stated goal of reforming an entire school district may be viewed as requiring several different agencies working in tightly coupled coordination to tackle different parts of the system.

The topics addressed in parts two and three, which focus on the actual tasks and the design and management of the partnership, are also important to discuss at the pre-partnership planning meeting. At the very least, the topics in part one should be discussed, because they constitute the foundation upon which all other partnership activities will be built.

## Step 4: Convene the Group: Identify Points of Congruence and Divergence

During planning group meetings, focus on fleshing out different views and assumptions about the core list of topics identified above. Once various interpretations and ideas regarding these topics are discussed, the group should focus on (1) areas in which participants' diverse skills and resources can be combined effectively, and (2) potential fault lines or disjunctures. Are there areas of agreement on which you can build, such as common notions of how best to design a professional-development workshop for middle-school math teachers? At this point in getting to know new partners, almost everyone will exhibit "first-date" politeness. It is important not to be too polite to disagree or to quickly assume that agreement on superficial features, such as apparent shared use of language or jargon, is sufficient grounds for collaborative work. You can probe more deeply while still on your best behavior by, for example, asking how each organization would respond to specific potential problems. Working through this exercise can reveal whether an apparent congruence is substantive and real.

If your meetings reveal that different organizations have fundamentally different views or theories about how to solve the problem, do not sidestep the issue. Such disagreements will need to be addressed. Can you turn these differences into opportunities for synergistic improvement, or are they show-stoppers? If the former, it is preferable to air these disagreements and plan how to manage them at this early stage. If the differences seem to be show-stoppers, it is also better to part amicably and look for a better match elsewhere than it is to proceed without knowledge of these potential deal breakers. Whether the planning meetings reveal congruence or divergence, it is important to begin developing a shared language among the partner organizations. This may entail defining certain terms that different groups might understand differently. (For example, mathematicians and math educators sometimes interpret the terms "explanation" and "problem" differently.) Some degree of consensus should be obtained about the specific problem being addressed by the partnership (e.g., improving math knowledge of middle-school teachers), the roles of different organizations and individuals, and the theories of action informing each participant.

### *Step 5: Think About How to Foster Innovation*

If your group is exploring an adaptive problem that will require a certain degree of innovation, you should consider how your partnership will foster this creativity while also achieving other goals. At least two things are important to create an environment that encourages innovation: adequate resources, and time and space devoted to creativity. Because innovation almost always requires more time, funding, personnel, and space than business as usual, consider how you will support innovation. Will you foster it during a series of brainstorming meetings by organizational representatives, or will you hold a specific working group responsible for it? Will it be a one time creative effort (e.g., designing a pamphlet) or a long-term process (e.g., developing new professional-development workshops for middle-school science teachers)? Whatever the particular situation, if your partnership will need innovative thinking or creativity to address complex educational problems, it is worth thinking about how these activities will unfold for you.

### *Step 6: Consider How Best to Proceed With the Partnership Planning*

Your planning group meetings may result in a number of scenarios. Writing a grant proposal or inking a memorandum of understanding can proceed immediately if there is sufficient agreement on the core topics. Or you might agree that the number and degree of differences are too great, and that the best option is to agree not to proceed. If you decide to move forward with the partnership, it is crucial at this stage to communicate clearly to all stakeholders the nature, rationale, and potential costs and benefits of the partnership (Tushnet, 1993). This is especially true for organizational leaders whose staff will be directly and substantively involved in the work. Ignoring this step raises the prospects that your staff or stakeholder groups will be taken by surprise by the partnership, will ask questions about why it is necessary, and will view partnership responsibilities as impinging on their daily tasks.

## A Final Word on Pre-Partnership Planning

Our recommendations for pre-partnership planning may appear to be too resource intensive or overly rational for some practitioners. If this relatively intensive process is not feasible for you, we still strongly urge you to conduct some sort of preliminary planning process or hold at least one stakeholder meeting. Skipping these pre-partnership planning meetings, and the discussion of the topics in the next three chapters, is a bit like jumping into a marriage without getting to know your spouse. It may work out, but do you really want to take that risk? The planning process should leave you well prepared to (a) determine whether you actually want to proceed with the partnership, and (b) design and manage the partnership effectively. Given the high stakes involved, taking these small steps toward getting to know your partners at the outset of the partnership will be time well spent.

You probably will need to repeat these steps at some point during your partnership, because circumstances will change and require you to revisit the partnership's goals, objectives, and tasks. This is a core process for managing partnerships in the unpredictable 3rd space—a process that can transform what can be an unsettling lack of familiarity and structure into an opportunity for learning and innovation. You and the other leaders should assess the partnership's progress regularly and deal proactively with new challenges and opportunities. Convening meetings with all major stakeholder groups, thereby ensuring that all contribute to possible solutions, is the best way to proceed.

## Chapter Summary

**Core Idea:** The details about a partnership's organizational structure and operational procedures should not be left unexplored or implicit but, instead, should be discussed clearly as a part of a deliberative planning process. By exploring crucial topics up front, potential partners can begin to establish personal relationships, identify areas of potential synergy, deepen partners' understanding of the problem being addressed, and uncover areas of disagreement that signal a need to forge some sort of consensus. Because the 3rd space of partnership is so unpredictable, it is also desirable to take this time to get to know your partners so you can develop some foresight about the road ahead.

### *Step 1: Select Participants for the Planning Group*

- Select a partner through funder requirements, existing professional or personal networks, or external conditions such as fiscal constraints.
- Convene your potential partners in one or more pre-partnership planning group meetings.
- Try to include representatives from all organizations and ensure that all participants are able to interact respectfully with people from diverse backgrounds and have the time to participate in a meaningful fashion.
- Include a program evaluator in your planning process to help articulate appropriate goals and objectives for your partnership. This will enhance your ability to provide compelling evidence about the effects of the partnership.

### *Step 2: Select an Objective and Skilled Facilitator*

- Select either a third party or one of the potential partners who can facilitate pre-partnership meetings effectively, ensure that they are efficiently run, and provide opportunities for all participants to safely voice their opinions.

### *Step 3: Come to the Meetings Prepared*

- Develop and circulate a list of key topics to be discussed at the meetings (Table 1).

- Before the planning meetings, hold intraorganizational meetings to discuss these topics, especially local assumptions about the nature of the problem to be addressed and about partnership work itself.

## Step 4: Convene the Group

- Discuss the key topics and examine areas in which participants' diverse skills and resources can be combined fruitfully as well as potential fault lines and disagreements.
- Develop a shared language regarding the work and a common framework for understanding each organization's role in the partnership.

## Step 5: Think About How to Foster Innovation

- If your partnership is addressing an adaptive problem, discuss how to allocate time, funding, and space to foster creativity and innovation.

## Step 6: Consider How Best to Proceed With the Partnership Planning

- Decide whether to proceed and develop a grant proposal or memorandum of understanding, or cease discussions about partnering.
- If you move forward, communicate to all stakeholders the partnership's value and potential costs to organizations, individuals, and the community.

## Bibliographic Note

The earliest analysis of the preliminary steps that practitioners should take when designing a partnership appeared in Barbara Intriligator's 1992 set of recommendations. Soon thereafter, Naida Tushnet published *A Guide to Developing Educational Partnerships* (1993), a thorough and insightful resource. For a description of a strategic planning process in the corporate world that strongly emphasizes which parties to engage, see Jim Collins's 2001 *Good to Great*. Our emphasis on using this pre-partnership planning process to build a sense of trust and familiarity draws on the work of Gray (1989) and Seely Brown and Duguid (2002).

# 2

# SIZING UP ORGANIZATIONAL ASPIRATIONS AND ATTRIBUTES

The most basic decision about starting a partnership is whether a partnership is actually the best vehicle for solving a particular problem. It is vital that all partners feel that a partnership, which will exact a toll on all participants' time, energy, and resources, is worthwhile and mutually beneficial. Thus, you need to answer the following questions before initiating a partnership: What goals does the partnership seek to achieve, and thus, what problems will it address? What are the specific objectives or tasks that will allow the partnership to achieve these goals? What are the motivations of the participating individuals and organizations? Does each partner actually have the material, human, and social resources to carry out the proposed activities? How autonomous does your organization need to be to remain in the partnership, and how closely linked do you want to be with others? Each of these topics should be discussed in your pre-partnership planning group. In this chapter we explore how these issues, when considered together, should affect the design and management of your partnership.

## Problems, Goals, and Objectives

For decades, educational researchers have exhorted partnership leaders to establish clear, achievable goals that all parties understand, and to ensure that each partner agrees on the problem to be solved and the proposed strategies to address the problem. Articulating shared goals and objectives is the first step toward creating a partnership-wide agreement about the problem to be addressed, how the problematic situation will be different if you succeed, and the tactics and activities that the partnership will undertake. In accomplishing this much, you are also fostering new relationships, opening new lines of communication, and identifying the organizational structure and procedures that need to be developed. We begin this section by considering the nature of problems and by defining goals and objectives. We then briefly consider the following attributes of shared goals and objectives: degree of agreement, suitability for partnership work, importance, alignment with partner constraints, clarity, and level of challenge. We conclude the section by considering the implications of goals and objectives for partnership success.

### *Identifying the Nature of the Problem: Technical or Adaptive?*

As we noted earlier, it is useful to determine whether the problem your partnership needs to resolve is a technical problem or an adaptive challenge. Your expectations about how much your goals and objectives will evolve will depend on which type of problem you tackle. In particular, the more adaptive your challenge, the more difficult it will be to define your goals and objectives clearly, and the more likely these are to evolve during the course of the partnership work. In addition, an adaptive challenge may complicate your program evaluation because goals and measurable objectives may not be apparent at first, which can complicate data collection efforts.

Another reason this distinction is useful is that your decisions about your organizational structure should differ depending on the degree to which your problem is technical or adaptive. When a partnership (or any organization) addresses a strictly technical problem, organizational structures should aim for broad implementation with high fidelity to the goals of the initiative. Organizational structures that maximize efficiency make sense because the problem and its solution, however complex, are understood, and procedures and roles do not need to be reinvented. Hence, more hierarchical systems are needed to implement a more tightly coupled organizational structure and protect the organization from disruption by outsiders who might cause staff to be distracted from the work at hand or might seek to redirect the organization's resources. However, when a partnership addresses a strongly emergent challenge, there is no set of defined procedures to implement, and efficient hierarchical organizational structures are likely to hinder rather than help. What is needed is a more flat and open organizational structure, in which nonauthoritarian boundary-crossers can mobilize the engagement of people with the different viewpoints and expertise needed to help the partnership better understand the problem and design promising objectives and strategies. The reality is that the problems most partnerships confront lie somewhere between the two extremes of a strictly technical problem and a fully emergent challenge. It is important to determine where on this continuum your problem lies.

> A technical problem is one that experts know how to identify, define, and solve. By contrast, an adaptive challenge is one that even the best experts have not clearly defined, let alone solved. Adaptive challenges require innovation and creativity and will likely take a long time to address adequately.

## *Defining Goals and Objectives*

A goal is a projected state of affairs that a person or an organization hopes to realize in the future (Locke & Latham, 2002). In programmatic terms, agreement on goals should follow from agreement on the problem to be addressed and should state how life will be different if an endeavor is successful. An example of a combined problem and goal statement is the following: "Science learning outcomes for students in a district X are unacceptably poor and will be measurably improved within five years." That is, the nature of the problem should inform the selected goals and objectives. The following are examples of some goals education partnerships typically seek:

- Improve student achievement in math and science at the elementary level.
- Introduce research-based teaching methods into introductory physics courses.
- Increase alignment between high school and undergraduate curricula.
- Revise a course sequence in mathematics for preservice teachers.

In most contexts, initial goal statements are quite broad and intentionally vague to allow many interpretations of the tactics necessary to address the problem. When the problem that the partners agree to address is a poorly understood adaptive challenge, this vagueness might be necessary: no one has clarity on the nature of such problems. Even when dealing with a well-understood technical problem, goal ambiguity is likely in the beginning, and goals alone are not sufficient grounds upon which to design and implement a partnership. This is where objectives come in. Objectives, although commonly considered to be the same as goals, are different. They identify specific tactics and activities that a group plans to use to reach the goal. The following are examples of objectives for each of the typical goals described above:

- Enroll all 45 elementary school teachers in inquiry-based science professional-development workshops.
- Within one year, have all instructors of introductory physics using clicker technology.
- Within two years, ensure that high school curricula address entrance requirements of local universities.
- Ensure that all courses in a preservice mathematics sequence get new textbooks and that all teaching assistants be trained in constructivist teaching methods.

Objectives delineate the specific strategies that will help a partnership achieve the projected state of affairs laid out in the goal statement. Identifying objectives also forces a discussion about the actual work of the partnership, that is, the tasks you will undertake to achieve the partnership's goals. For instance, what specific activities will take place in the inquiry-based science professional-development workshops? Will the workshops emphasize hands-on experimentation or more conceptual learning? Will the workshops last one day or one week? In thinking through your objectives, you must also consider issues related to partner roles, responsibilities, and theories of action. As a result, all of the partners also should agree on objectives at both the conceptual and the logistical levels. As with goals, when dealing with objectives, each partner will be constrained regarding which activities it can commit to, based on resources and preexisting structures, policies, and routines.

Also bear in mind that goals, and hence objectives, can change, particularly if you identify a problem that is strongly adaptive in nature. Thus, a key element of the partnership work is to hammer out new understandings of the nature of the problem being addressed. But even if the problem you identify is largely technical, changing circumstances and conditions will probably require you to revise your goals and objectives (Sirotnik & Goodlad, 1988). Thus, most partnership leaders find that their initial goals need revision, often several times. For example, the science professional-development group within UDEP found that its initial goal of improving teacher understanding of scientific concepts needed to be stated much more clearly to get all of the parties on board, particularly teachers who desired a specific statement of what the partnership was intending to do. Stay open to the possibility that you will need to revise your goals in response to better understanding of the problem and emerging circumstances.

A program evaluator can provide invaluable help in identifying goals and objectives at the early stage of and throughout the process, as can someone with expertise in project management. These professionals will be able to help you establish clear and measurable objectives that are aligned with your goals. In addition to helping you make detailed plans, they can help you design specific activities that will enable you to meet your objectives and provide data that show staff, funders, and other stakeholders that you are in fact achieving the project's goals.

## *Important Attributes of Partnership Problems, Goals, and Objectives*

We now consider specific attributes of shared goals and objectives as they relate to the success of partnerships. The first of these attributes is *degree of agreement* on the problem, goals, and objectives. Let's say the partners agree that teacher professional-development is the problem to work on. You will probably be more successful if you agree on the causes of this problem. Are the professional development courses aligned with what teachers need to learn? Is the prevailing teaching approach as effective as it could be in light of emerging research in the learning sciences? If you are considering a policy-induced partnership, in which the funder identifies the problems, are you certain that all of the potential partners take these problems seriously enough to warrant the costs of a partnership? The more fully you and your potential partners agree on the problem to be addressed (as well as on the technical versus adaptive nature of the problem), the more likely it is that you will agree on partnership goals and objectives.

Agreement on the goals and objectives also is essential to partnership success. In businesses, agreement on goals and objectives sometimes is known as corporate vision. The lack of a common understanding of the problem, goals, and objectives is a common reason why many collaborations and partnerships fail (see Accenture, 1999), thus undermining the effectiveness of work in the 3rd space. It is particularly important to agree on objectives, which specify the nature of the work to be conducted, so you can ensure that the proposed activities are feasible within the constraints of existing organizational structures and policies, and that the tasks are suitable for achieving the partnership's goals.

A second attribute is *suitability for partnership work*. Some problems are better addressed without a partnership, whereas others can be resolved successfully only by multiple organizations working together. For example, a small committee of mathematics faculty can probably revise the list of required courses for mathematics majors, whereas revision of the basic calculus courses that students in a variety of majors throughout a university must take might require the participation of faculty from engineering, statistics, and other departments. Thus, you need to determine whether the problem you are addressing, and hence the goals you are seeking to meet, needs a partnership. Starting a partnership requires a substantial investment of time, money, and energy; you need to determine up front whether you should embark on a partnership at all.

A third attribute is the *importance* of your goals and objectives. Are the goals sufficiently valuable to each partner to warrant the inevitable costs of developing and managing a partnership? To assess the value an organization places on the goal under discussion and the likelihood that the organization can deliver on its promises, make sure that the objectives under discussion align with each organization's prevailing activities. If they do not, the partnership you endeavor to create will represent a departure from normal procedures, which may present difficulties for that organization's staff and leadership.

It is also useful to consider the *alignment* of goals and objectives with the different partner organizations' constraints. For instance, a proposal to introduce new teaching methods into undergraduate physics courses might or might not be feasible depending on the policies of a particular physics department, the perspectives of the department chair or others in positions of influence, and other structural considerations. Similarly, K–12 districts, which operate under many constraints over which they have little control, may simply not be able to pursue a goal even if individuals within the districts strongly agree that the goal is important. If a partnership's goals and objectives are poorly aligned with an organization's mission and daily operations, that organization's commitment to the partnership may erode when it is asked to provide the promised staff time or other resources or when conflict arises. Consider, for example, a university that does not view science instruction in middle schools as central to its mission but nevertheless participates in a partnership focused on that topic out of a general commitment to public education. If this partnership requires the university to devote significant staff time and resources to improving middle-school science instruction, staff and faculty may question the importance of the partnership work.

A fifth attribute is *clarity*. Your goals and objectives should be sufficiently well defined, specific, and understood that participants will not question why they are involved when they experience the inevitable problems that emerge from collective work. Indeed, the process of identifying clearly stated and shared goals, in and of itself, has strong effects on individual psychology and motivation. Research on organizational behavior has identified cognitive mechanisms that connect goal setting and performance: individuals appraise what types of behavior they should engage in based on established goals, how much effort should be spent, and how challenges or failures will be dealt with (Stajkovic, Locke, & Blair, 2006). This same research has demonstrated that goals affect performance by directing attention and effort toward relevant activities, energizing the actor, influencing persistence, and possibly leading to the discovery of task-specific knowledge. Activating these positive emotions will make your goal easier to reach. Thus, having clear and well-understood goals will influence not only the partnership as a whole but also the motivations and effectiveness of the individuals working on particular projects.

In addition to increasing motivation and group function, clearly stated goals and objectives also provide program evaluators with something concrete to work with. All of the objectives listed earlier under "Defining Goals and Objectives" include specific and measurable objectives (e.g., "Within two years, ensure that high school curricula address entrance requirements of local universities"). Concrete objectives provide an evaluator with benchmarks by which to assess a program's success, which is especially important in the face of increasing demands for researchers and evaluators to produce robust and compelling evidence for program efficacy.

*Level of challenge* is the final important attribute of goals and objectives. Your goals should be sufficiently difficult that they cannot be accomplished without collaboration among the partners. But if they are extremely difficult to achieve, you may fail. The partnership we studied set a goal that was extremely difficult to achieve: improve performance for 100% of the students in several urban districts. One UDEP leader noted, "We had lots of goals that were ambitious and beyond what we could have delivered on." This led the leaders to launch overly ambitious activities, and as it became clear that targets were not being achieved, the project lost credibility with some people on the ground, and the leaders had to explain why they failed to achieve certain goals. Thus, it is important to consider the level of difficulty and complexity of your goals and objectives in light of their feasibility: Are they within the sphere of influence of the partnership? Do the participants have enough resources and time? The goals not only must be suitable for partnership and sufficiently valued and clear, but also must be challenging enough to warrant the effort and other costs that partnerships inevitably entail and still be within reach.

---

**Partnership Action Point:** Ensure that all goals and objectives are in alignment with the nature of the problem to be addressed and the particular needs and capabilities of relevant partner organizations.

---

## Agenda Items for Your Pre-Partnership Meeting

Discussion of goals and objectives will have at least two significant implications for the overall good of a partnership. One concerns the process itself: this process should open lines of communication among partners and clarify the nature of the cultural models that are in play. The discussion about goals and objectives probably will conjure up a variety of different perspectives on, for example, how best to improve physics courses or align curricula. The second, less well-understood, implication is that the problems, goals, and objectives you identify affect partnership organizational structure. Whether you are dealing with a technical problem or one that is more adaptive, the complexity and types of strategies, the length of time needed, and the number of organizations required to achieve these goals are all factors that should be considered when you choose an organizational structure and design your procedures (Intriligator, 1982). As a case in point, the more adaptive the problem, the more important it will be to have multiple voices and areas of expertise at the table, less hierarchy, and more collaboration. Let's say your problem is persistent weak student performance in science, associated with poor teacher preparation. This is an adaptive problem—experts continue to fail to address this problem effectively. Your objective is that university faculty and district staff will work together to construct new curricular units, test them in pilots, train teachers across the district to use them, and simultaneously seek to curb teacher turnover. In this case, your partnership is facing a long-term, complex challenge that requires intense collaboration among the partners. In such cases, you will need to set up organizational structures that support true collaboration, whereby each partner contributes skills and knowledge and works interdependently with the others—thus relinquishing some autonomy—to achieve shared goals.

On the other hand, let's say your problem is to add units to a K–12 district where a particular curriculum is already being used (a more technical problem) and your objective is that universities will develop these units and provide them to a professional-development organization to deliver to districts. In this case, your partnership is taking on a more discrete challenge that requires coordination but not intensive collaboration. In such a case, in which the different partners play relatively independent roles in a supply chain, you should set up organizational structures that largely maintain each partner's autonomy and require only minimal interdependence. (See Table 2 in chapter 5 for a quick guide to selecting organizational structures.) In sum, if you do *not* carefully articulate your shared problem, goals, and objectives in the pre-partnership period, you will be less likely to identify an appropriate organizational structure, set up a high-quality evaluation, effectively motivate and inspire your staff, and prepare the way for effective relationship building within the 3rd space of partnership.

## Motivations

Related to goals and objectives are the motivations each organization and individual has for participating in the partnership. It is important to understand all partners' motivations for engaging in a partnership, not to judge them, but to maximize the likelihood that your partnership will succeed. While healthy self-interest should be an element of every partner's motivation, the partners should know up front whether any partner is not also strongly motivated to improve conditions for the partnership as a whole. Knowing what your potential partners hope to gain—at the organizational, group, and individual levels—will give you insights into their levels of commitment and what each expects from the others. It also will help you make better decisions about the type of partnership arrangement you should choose. First, we briefly discuss different types of motivations for partnering and the important role of enlightened self-interest. We then consider how motivations, like goals and objectives, point toward particular organizational structures and procedures.

### Types of Motivation for Initiating a Partnership

Organizational researchers have long been interested in examining the reasons why organizations enter into partnerships, especially because these reasons tend to predict partnership success and performance. Early research conceptualized motivations as falling roughly into one of two groups: symmetrical reasons (all parties are motivated by a desire to attain goals collectively) and asymmetrical reasons (one organization would prefer to remain autonomous but external forces or coercion lead it to interact). The role of the external environment, particularly market forces that are beyond the control of any single organization, has long been an important area of research. This emphasis is partly in response to the growing recognition that organizations change and adapt to external forces. In this vein, Oliver (1990) reviewed the literature and identified the following six major reasons why organizations decide to partner with one another:

- necessity, to conform with legal or regulatory requirements;
- asymmetry, to exercise control or power over another organization;
- reciprocity, to pursue common interests or mutually beneficial goals;
- efficiency, to improve organizational efficiency by streamlining operations;
- stability, to stabilize the organization in response to an environmental uncertainty; and
- legitimacy, to increase organizational legitimacy to appear in agreement with prevailing norms or expectations of the external environment.

These different types of motivations demonstrate the diversity of rationales that may be leading your partners to consider interacting with you and your organization. Instead of assuming that people are motivated by a benign sense of reciprocity or ignoring motivations altogether, it is worth considering each of these motivation types and identifying which types may be at play in your particular situation.

### The Role of Self-Interest: Beware of Too Much and Too Little

Self-interest is a necessary component of successful collaborations because it ensures that the home organization's interests will be protected. Self-interest ensures that "each needs the others to advance their individual interests," thus increasing the incentive to work through the inevitable challenges associated with partnership to achieve success (Gray, 1989, p. 6). However, it could be a problem if a potential partner's *only* motivation to join the partnership is self-interest. If this person or entity participates at all, it should be as an independent contractor or in some other role that establishes distance between it and the rest of the partnership. Similarly, you may find situations in which an organization is motivated to partner primarily to advance its own status, profits, or mission. In such a situation, you should recognize that this partner has a high need for organizational autonomy and should keep it at arm's length. For example, Tushnet (1993) describes a partnership whose goal was to transform classrooms from teacher-centered to learner-centered environments. One partner was a technology company that provided equipment and joined with the clear motivation to increase market share for its products. In this case, the fact that the company's primary motivation was self-interest did not harm the well-being of the collective because the partner operated at arm's length; it only provided equipment and was not involved at the level of implementation that required true collaboration among partners.

At the other extreme are situations in which a partner is motivated almost entirely by an altruistic desire to advance the well-being of communities beyond itself. Be aware that such a partner may have too little motivation based on self-interest to keep going when things get challenging. This happened with the preservice math committee of the UDEP partnership. Some of the mathematicians joined this group because they believed it would provide them with an effective way to contribute to the public good. When they found themselves in situations in which the other partners presented them with mental models that confounded them, they became frustrated and decided the partnership was not worth it. Again, if the partnership structure keeps groups such as this at a distance, perhaps through a limited partnership, then this potential loss of interest can be mitigated. That said, some degree of altruism or interest in improving the public good is important, indeed is a core component of *enlightened self-interest*. Partners motivated by enlightened self-interest seek to advance their own interests and believe they can achieve this aim as they simultaneously enhance the lives and interests of broader entities, such as a K–12 district or a city's population as a whole. While enlightened self-interest is not a requirement of partnership, it is a highly promising motivation for education partnerships, which by their very nature focus on improving the lives of students or the general population.

## Agenda Items for Your Pre-Partnership Meeting

Two points pertaining to motivations are especially relevant to discuss at your pre-partnership planning meetings. One is that individual participants' motivations are complex: everyone will have to balance multiple and competing obligations once they begin working in the 3rd space of partnership.

Partnerships are designed and implemented by individuals who function in a variety of roles, each of which entails different loyalties and obligations (Intriligator, 1982). For instance, a K–12 school principal will participate as a representative of and advocate for his or her own school, a supporter of the partnership, and an individual with his or her own personal goals. It is important to recognize that these different obligations may work at cross-purposes at times, leading individuals to make some decisions that are not in the best interest of the collective. Some people participate in a partnership at significant risk to their own self-interest. For example, research university faculty who take time to work on a partnership project give up time they otherwise would devote to writing articles for journals or conducting research, the two activities primarily rewarded in their departments. In fact, tenure decisions about some faculty who participated in the UDEP project were jeopardized because of their perceived lack of research accomplishments and the not so subtle complaint that they spent too much time on "outreach" and "service," which is how their partnership activity was categorized.

> **Partnership Action Point:** The different obligations an individual has toward his or her home organization and to the partnership may not always be in accord and may ultimately work at cross-purposes, leading individuals to make decisions that are not in the best interests of the collective.

The other point pertains to the fact that external funding agencies often initiate the formation of education partnerships. Regardless of whether potential partners are motivated by altruism, strong self-interest, or enlightened self-interest, the prospect of grant funding alters the picture, because the grant acts as a resource base that either brings different groups and individuals together in the first place or allows an existing partnership to expand or continue beyond its planned period. In the former case, a common outcome is a "marriage of convenience," wherein partners join forces less out of a mutual recognition of one another's value or a commonly held vision for change than out of a need to satisfy funder requirements (Waschak & Kingsley, 2006). Some of these marriages of convenience are based on commonly held theories of action and strong mutual need and produce substantial value for the partners. However, when partners select one another primarily because they help each other meet funding agency criteria, and not primarily on the basis of a commonly held theory of action or mutual need, the funder mandate ends up fostering partnerships that are not likely to succeed. Further, it is important to recognize that the funder's cultural models for addressing problems may need to be accomodated or otherwise incorporated into the partnership effort.

## Capacity and Resources

Thoughtfully developed shared goals and strong agreement on strategies and theories may amount to little if the partners do not have the capacity needed to implement the strategies. Before you enter a partnership, it is ideal to have reliable information about the nature of the resources each partner will commit to the partnership and whether the resulting combination of available resources is sufficient to achieve the partnership goals. If you discover that the required resources are not available, then you can determine how to obtain them to move the partnership forward. Below we discuss the types of resources you should think about up front.

### *Types of Organizational Capacity and Resources to Consider*

Organizational capacity refers to the ability of an organization to use its resources and skills successfully to accomplish its goals. An organization's resource capacity is not limited to material resources (e.g., the size of its buildings or its budget) but also includes human and social resources. We draw on the work of Gamoran et al. (2003) to distinguish among the following three types of organizational resources:

- *Material resources*: Items that can be exchanged between groups, including money, information technology, curricula, or other physical objects, are considered material resources. These resources can also be used to generate new material resources of their own, including a new influx of funding.
- *Human resources*: The skills and knowledge of organizational members represent an important human resource that individuals and organizations can exchange. For instance, in education partnerships university faculty are commonly viewed as resources for content knowledge, and K–12 faculty are commonly viewed as resources for pedagogical knowledge. The extent of an organization's investment in its own staff may indicate the strength and depth of its human resources.

- *Social resources*: The roles and relationships individuals and groups bring to a partnership represent an important social resource. In addition, as different groups come together, they create their own social resources, including new cultural models and ways of interacting with one another, which may in turn provide a new resource for future efforts (Gamoran et al., pp. 26–27).

When combined, these resources represent the capacity of an organization to perform a given action and should be taken into account when assessing how well an organization can meet the needs of a partnership. Do the partners have adequate staffing or funding to achieve the goals or actually to implement the tasks necessary to meet the stated objectives? Consider these hard questions up front, hand in hand with your consideration of goals and objectives.

## *A Focus on Social Resources: Embedded Relationships*

We call attention here to one aspect of social resources that can exert a particularly strong influence on a partnership: existing, or embedded, relationships with other groups. Embedded relationships that each partner organization has with the other partners and with other, nonpartner organizations—whether positive or negative—are a core part of the partners' identities and operations and will influence the partnership. If you know whether these embedded relationships are positive or negative, how strong they are, and which people within each organization they involve, you are much more likely to be able to use them strategically and much less likely to run into unanticipated, awkward, or even damaging situations.

### *Positive Embedded Relationships*

Individuals and organizations that see new opportunities for collaborative work probably will seek potential partners from the ranks of individuals, projects, or organizations they already trust and respect. In other words, you choose to build on positive embedded relationships. In situations like this, the process of developing a working relationship is likely to be smoother and less time-consuming because the participants are probably sufficiently familiar with one another that they already have a shared language and understanding of how to work with one another. In our study, the science professional-development group benefited tremendously from the positive embedded relationship that had developed among local K–12 and IHE leaders during the implementation of two prior grants with goals similar to

UDEP's goals for improving science education. This group benefited from existing networks among district personnel and between a few local university faculty and district leaders who already trusted each other and knew how to work together.

---

**Partnership Action Point:** Do not assume that an effective partnership will automatically flow from a previously existing relationship with a colleague or an organization.

---

However, do not assume that an effective partnership will inevitably result just because you have a positive embedded relationship with another partner. The trust and shared language needed for new partnerships may not flow automatically from positive prior relations. Indeed, a downside to relying on preexisting relationships is that you may incorrectly assume that individuals or groups with whom you get along well in, say, social situations or community activities, will be trustworthy and compatible as members of an education partnership. In addition, prior relationships may not be transferrable. That is, a cross-organizational relationship that worked for one project or partnership may not work as well for a subsequent project or in different branches of the partners' networks. Another reason to be careful about apparently positive embedded relationships is that these often are a package deal, because these preexisting ties also come with additional baggage. For example, partners who have embedded relations with their target population may also have a local reputation that an outside observer might find difficult to discern. In addition, you will also be inheriting the group's specific theories of action and strategies for addressing particular problems, which probably will exert a strong influence on the partnership's activities.

*Negative Embedded Relationships*

Education partnerships typically involve large numbers of people and organizations, making it likely that some damaged relationships predate a new partnership. These negative embedded relationships, which can exert a powerful influence on a partnership, should be identified as quickly as possible. They may be signaled by such evidence as one partner's immediate suspicion of another group's motives for partnering, eye rolling and other expressions of disrespect, or comments suggesting that all of the individuals from the other partner are infected by bad blood between the organizations. For example, one member of the science professional-development group reported that the K–12 district had long harbored a sense of mistrust toward the other local universities. In the opinion of some teacher participants, the teacher-training programs at the IHEs were inadequate, in part because of recalcitrant faculty who refused to adopt research-based teaching methods that would improve preservice students' content knowledge. This led to little desire or incentive to collaborate with local IHEs. One teacher summed up this tension by expressing her frustration on learning that she would be working closely with a particular faculty member in a summer workshop: "I took a class from him, and I hated it. I can't believe he's going to be co-facilitating with us!"

To avoid being surprised by such a sentiment, try to identify flash points based on preexisting antagonisms quickly and work to avoid or mitigate interactions that will hinder the development of trust among the partners. For example, if you plan to bring together K–12 teachers and higher education faculty, you should ask if any of the participants have an unusually positive or negative personal history with someone from the other group. If this is the case, instead of randomly assigning individuals to working teams, group people who seem most likely to be aware of one another's cultural models and more able to work effectively together.

## *Agenda Items for Your Pre-Partnership Meetings*

In partnerships, it is important to identify as clearly as possible the organizational capacity each partner organization (including your own) brings to the table and how much of that capacity is available for the collective. This requires organizational leaders to be willing to share openly and honestly precisely what their organization is capable of contributing to the partnership. Each potential partner needs to share information not only about the resources it has but also about the degree to which it can make its resources available for use within the 3rd space of partnership. Several members of the UDEP partnership were unhappily surprised, once the partnership got under way, that they had greatly overestimated their partners' capacity to provide the needed resources. Regarding social resources, it also is very important to surface, and consider the implications of, embedded relationships.

### Autonomy and Interdependence

We had ongoing relationships with K–12 districts
that preexisted the partnership, and that would
likely postexist it, so in our minds UDEP had to

fit into what we were doing in these districts and
not add any noise or problems. We have a theory of action based on providing districts a
coherent and integrated set of recommendations and professional development, and so
we're really careful to monitor who talks to the
district staff. We may have looked like we were
being gatekeepers when what we were trying to
do was be true to our theory of action.

(UDEP participant)

One of the defining characteristics of partnership is that each partner organization takes on a dual identity. It maintains its home organization identity
while acquiring an identity as a member of the new entity. This dual identity
embodies the tension between self-interest (achieving individual organizational missions) and a collective interest (achieving collaboration goals and
maintaining accountability to collaborative partners and their stakeholders)
(Thomson & Perry, 2006). This creative tension promotes synergy within
partnerships.

### Agenda Items for Your Pre-Partnership Meetings

The concept of loosely and tightly coupled systems is useful for thinking
about how to identify and manage this tension. Organizations, including
partnerships, can be described in terms of how loosely or tightly their various
subsystems are coupled (e.g., departments or colleges). Organizational scientist Karl Weick (1976) suggests that coupling refers not only to linkages and
connections among administrative units but also to the degree to which each
unit maintains its own identity and autonomy. Weick argues that schools
and universities are loosely coupled organizations in which different units
such as departments operate with relative autonomy and do not follow an
organization-wide rationale for procedures such as decision making. Loosely
coupled systems are characterized by infrequent contacts and weak connec-
tions between individuals in different units. An example of a very loosely
coupled system is a university that favors departmental governance so that
political turmoil in one department will have little impact on another. You
must decide how loosely or tightly coupled you want to be with the other
individuals and organizations in your partnership.

While it is important to negotiate the tension between self-interest and
the interests of the collective for the entire duration of a partnership, it is

especially crucial to deal with this tension at the beginning. To do this, it is helpful to consider both your home organization and the proposed partnership in terms of Weick's concept of tight and loose coupling. First, determine the degree of autonomy your home organization needs. Take time to stake out your own organizational (and personal) self-interests and to identify your boundaries. Second, consider the degree of coupling the partnership will need to achieve its goals. For instance, a goal to provide a laptop for every child in a district may not require that the computer manufacturer, the district, and technical support become a tightly coupled organization. On the other hand, achieving the goal of improving preservice and inservice teacher training by simultaneously introducing the same new pedagogical methods and curricular material in both settings probably will require a high level of interdependence. Third, consider whether your home organization's need for autonomy is aligned with the degree of interdependence the partnership will require. Decide how much power and turf each organization needs to relinquish to achieve the partnership's goals, and whether your organization can do this. Based on these considerations, you are much more likely to make workable decisions about organizational structures and procedures.

## Agenda Items for Your Pre-Partnership Meetings

Organizational autonomy and interdependence issues will substantially influence whether you should proceed with a partnership and, if so, how you should structure your partnership. During the pre-partnership period, you should try to answer the following three questions associated with organizational interdependence: Will the proposed partnership preserve and extend, or potentially help or hurt, your home organization? What boundaries should you place between your organization and the partnership? How will the potential partners meet the challenges of attribution (a term we explain below)?

### Will the Partnership Work Help or Hurt Your Organization?

You need to consider whether the partnership might end up damaging your home organization's core activity. A partnership should enhance and not impinge upon these activities, so that the time and energy the partnership exacts is worth the effort. Self-interest is a necessary component of successful partnerships, because it must be clear to all organizational members that the benefits will outweigh the inevitable costs. If the partnership's goals conflict with those of your organization, then your organization's reputation and the quality of its work will be at risk. Without a firm conviction on the part of organizational leaders that self-interest is being preserved, and actually enhanced, the chances that the partnership will succeed are lessened. Further, some types of partnerships, particularly collaborative ones that involve high degrees of interdependence, require leaders to consider their partners' self-interest as well. Sirotnik and Goodlad (1988) suggest that a key component of the symbiotic relationship that characterizes a collaborative partnership is "a mutual satisfaction of self-interest, and sufficient selflessness on the part of each member to assure the satisfaction of self interests on the part of all members" (p. 14).

*What Boundaries Should You Place Between Your Organization and the Partnership?*

You also need to determine which aspects of each partner organization are subject to influence by the partnership and which are off limits. Every organization has some activities and territory that must remain outside the partnership domain. For example, it is unlikely that a university department would allow a K–12 partner to become involved in tenure decisions, just as few K–12 districts would allow a university faculty member to make district budgetary decisions. Areas that are off limits must be demarcated and publicly acknowledged so all parties understand and appreciate them. For those activities that fall within the shared partnership space, decisions must be made about what relationship each partner will have to those activities, how much decision-making power will be shared across organizations, and which people will have decision-making authority. In sum, partners must clearly stake out what is common territory of a partnership, and thus subject to joint decision making and scrutiny, and what is not. If these boundaries are not communicated clearly, they can become a flash point for conflict. This step is also important in determining which organizational structures and procedures are most appropriate in the 3rd space. For instance, if there is little interest in collective action, and organizations hold tightly to their own turf, the partnership should be structured in a way that requires less interdependence and collective decision making.

---

**Partnership Action Point:** Areas that are off limits for the partnership must be demarcated and publicly acknowledged so all parties understand and appreciate them.

*How Will You Meet the Challenges of Attribution?*

At some point, a partnership will need to report activities and allocate credit for the work, whether to the community being served, policy makers and funders, or an internal governing body. At that time, it will be necessary to decide what should be claimed as collective work and labeled as such. This decision should flow naturally once the partnership boundaries are demarcated, because it will be clear which work is strictly one partner's and cannot be claimed as partnership work and which work lies in the collective space. Factors to take into account when deciding what can be claimed as partnership work include which organization has the most at stake, where the work actually takes place, and how claiming a particular outcome for the partnership will influence the perception of the partnership and local ownership. It is important to demonstrate respect for the local work and to encourage ownership; to claim specific efforts as work of the partnership, and not of the local organization, may send an unintended message that the local work is unimportant. In the UDEP project, some K–12 district staff felt that the professional-development efforts the partnership supported were district accomplishments that the partnership was simply building on. When the partnership leaders claimed this as partnership work, the K–12 staff felt that this minimized the district's investment and ownership and provided yet another example of outside agencies claiming credit for the hard work that goes on in schools. It is possible, though, that once a partnership develops and a collective identity is forged among various organizations, the local organization may be more willing to cede "naming rights" and begin calling the work "partnership work."

## Chapter Summary

**Core Idea:** The nature of the problem, goals, and objectives; motivations for partnering; organizational capacity; and interdependence are four crucial topics that must be considered carefully in the beginning stages of partnership planning. The process of discussing these topics will suggest appropriate organizational structures and procedures, reveal areas of overlap and potential conflict among the potential partners, and begin to open lines of communication and build camaraderie.

## Problems, Goals, and Objectives

- Problems should be agreed on and identified on the continuum between technical problems and emergent challenges.
- Agreement on goals should follow from agreement on the problem to be addressed.
- Objectives should be specific and measurable, while also setting forth the specific tasks that will lead the group to realizing its goals.
- Goals and objectives are important to motivate staff, inform evaluation, and provide a road map.
- Key attributes of partnership goals and objectives are the degree of agreement on the problem, goals, and objectives; suitability for partnership; importance; alignment with partner constraints; clarity; and level of challenge.

## Motivations

- The rationale for engaging in partnership will suggest particular organizational structures.
- Self-interest is a necessary component of partnership, but each participant should also have some commitment to the well-being of the collective.

## Capacity and Resources

- Include material resources, human resources (e.g., skills and knowledge), in organizational capacity and social resources (e.g., networks)
- Understand what different parties can actually accomplish and which of their resources are available for use by the partnership

## Autonomy and Interdependence

- Identify how tightly or loosely coupled you wish to be with other individuals and organizations.
- Think first about preserving your own self-interest.

## Agenda Items for Your Pre-Partnership Meetings

- Discuss the nature of your problem, goals and objectives, motivations, resource availability, and the degree of desired autonomy interdependence among partners.
- Insights into these matters lay the groundwork for future relationships and suggest appropriate organizational structures for your partnership.

## Bibliographic Note

Several researchers, including Sirotnik and Goodlad (1988) and Tushnet (1993), encourage partnership designers and managers to ensure that all parties have a common understanding of the partnership's problem, goals, and specific activities. For case studies that emphasize the unpredictable nature of partnership and the potential for revising or updating your goals and objectives, see Houck, Cohn, and Cohn (2004). Several of the books and articles on education partnership included in the bibliographic note for the introduction also focus on the topics covered in this chapter.

For a discussion of the different attributes of goals that are related to successful collaborative work, see *Harnessing Complexity* by Axelrod and Cohen (2000). Research on goals and task performance has a long history in organizational behavior, which is closely related to industrial and organizational psychology. See Locke and Latham (2002) for a primer on the relationship of goal setting to task performance and Stajkovic et al. (2006) for a more recent analysis. Oliver (1990) provides a good overview of the organizational science literature on motivation, and Schmidt and Kuchan (1977) provide insights into the relationship between motivations and collaboration outcomes. For a focus on how external forces such as fiscal crises or federal policy mandates can influence organizations, see the seminal work of DiMaggio and Powell (1983) on institutional theory. For an overarching analysis of collaborations that addresses some of the topics in this chapter, consult Barbara Gray's excellent 1989 book, *Collaborating: Finding Common Ground for Multiparty Problems*.

For a review of the different types of resources required to conduct a partnership adequately (i.e., material, human, social) as they pertain to teaching reform, see Gamoran et al. (2003). The notion of embeddedness is based on Mark Granovetter's seminal work (1973). For an astute analysis of how embeddedness affects education partnerships, see Slater (2004) and Waschak and Kingsley (2006). For a discussion of tight and loose coupling in organizations, see Weick (1976), and for an analysis of coupling in higher education, see Birnbaum (1991). Finally, for analyses of the role of organizational autonomy and boundaries, see Ring and Van de Ven (1994) and Thomson and Perry (2006).

# 3

# UNDERSTANDING
# CULTURAL DYNAMICS

When I went to give the first presentation on
UDEP at the request of the Mathematics Department, one of the faculty got up and yelled at me
and said this was a waste of money and that this
had no relevance to the department. And
another came over and sat down next to me and
said, after audibly sniffing in my direction,
"Eeyiu, educationalese."

(UDEP participant)

The fact that the prevailing cultural dynamics of K–12 schools, IHEs,
and other organizations will influence your efforts to create a partnership in the unpredictable 3rd space is a core message of this
book. Individuals coming into the partnership will have preexisting ideas
and notions about topics as varied as collaboration, teaching, and education
reform, and each of these mental models will inform how the partnership
is structured and implemented. Within each organization, collections of
mental models (i.e., cultural models) inform organizational structures and
are reinforced through relationships and routines that contribute to the
sense that "this is how we do things." Knowledge of these preexisting cultural models, and the specific affinity groups to which they are connected
(e.g., a high school math department), will help you anticipate and negotiate the tensions and conflicts that inevitably come with partnerships.

Why focus on the relationship between culture and conflict? Nearly
every book or article on education partnerships refers to the challenges of
working with individuals from different organizational and disciplinary cultures. The disparate participants in a given partnership may include science

and education faculty, higher education and K–12 faculty, and teachers and administrators, many of whom speak different technical languages; have different workplace norms; and, most important, hold some stereotypes about and perhaps harbor resentment toward one another. For instance, K–12 teachers and administrators accustomed to working under firm and tight deadlines may be frustrated with university counterparts, who might work under more flexible deadlines and who are expected to engage continuously in exploration and dialogue. In education partnerships that involve close contact among these groups, such differences in expectations and routines can lead to conflict and misunderstanding and derail even the best-laid partnership plans. Thus, the frequency and intensity of tensions that might arise should not be underestimated.

> **Partnership Action Point:** Knowledge of the cultural dynamics prevailing in each home organization and its affinity groups will help you anticipate and negotiate the tensions and conflicts that inevitably come with partnerships.

Other aspects of culture will inevitably affect your partnership as well. Factors such as ethnicity, gender, and power probably influence the cultural dynamics within each of the home organizations in your partnership. For instance, there may be some history of gender discrimination toward female tenure-track faculty in a university physics department or an intense power struggle within a K–12 district administration. It is desirable to understand these internal dynamics and assess them in conjunction with partnership-specific issues, so you can ascertain the compatibility of the different groups involved and any potential trouble areas *prior to* entering into a partnership.

Two types of cultural dynamics will affect the partnership you plan to create. One type is broad in scope and includes the larger contexts in which each of the home organizations operates, including attributes of each one's geographic, political, and economic contexts. For example, educational policy at the national, state, and local levels and economic conditions related to educational funding are part of the broader environment in which schools, districts, and IHEs operate. Then there are the structural and sociocultural contexts that historically have influenced education, including the hierarchical relationships that prevail across—and within—the higher education and K–12 sectors, and the value-laden relationships associated with the hard and soft sciences. Over time, different views on these dynamics have become cultural models for particular groups, such as the not uncommon view that hard sciences are more robust and "scientific" than soft sciences.

The other type of cultural dynamic, and the one that is the focus of this chapter, is internal to each organization and refers to the specific cultural models, relationships, structure and technologies, and routines and practices of different affinity groups within each partner organization. Successful partnering requires being able to work with diverse affinity groups from various organizations and to foster meaningful interactions so that the different skills, assets, and insights each group brings to the table can synergize. This is not an easy task; it is often characterized by miscommunication and a lack of familiarity with one another's ways of thinking and working. But by acknowledging how each organization is constrained and enabled by its particular cultural context, and identifying the specific cultural models, structures, technologies, and routines with which its members make sense of the world, you will be well equipped to deal with cultural dynamics that are an inherent aspect of partnerships.

We then consider the opportunities inherent in partnership work for creating the conditions for new cultural dynamics to unfold. The optimal partnership process is *not* to forge a common culture, whereby each organization melts into a new, single identity; teachers and administrators need to maintain their original identities with their school or IHE. However, if partnership work is carefully designed, productive, and meaningful to its participants, a partnership can create a new sense of shared purpose and affiliation among the different organizations involved. We focus on how partnership structures, relationships, and practices can be developed to increase the prospects for generating new and productive cultural models.

## Avoiding the Common-Culture Myth

When talking about cultural phenomena in K–12 schools or IHEs, people often assume that norms or beliefs uniformly apply to all members of a group (e.g., a department) or even the entire organization, forgetting that even in the smallest organization there exists much diversity of opinion, belief, and practice. For instance, in our analysis of the UDEP partnership, we frequently came across the characterization that all K–12 teachers are attuned to frequent and short deadlines and the pressures of a busy day, and university faculty are more accustomed to leisurely exploration and accomplishing tasks with few outside pressures. While it may be possible to attribute to an entire organization a particular feature such as a story or saga that helps define it, cultural life in organizations is far more complex.

> Culture is too complex and multifaceted to allow for labeling an entire organization as a particular "type" of culture. Instead, a school or an IHE may have a variety of different affinity groups that share different cultural models and relationships, occupy different structural niches, and engage in different daily practices.

There may be an element of truth to some generalizations; it is undeniable, for example, that K–12 teachers and university faculty have substantially different demands on their time. But to characterize an entire group or organization based on these superficial differences masks subtle and important differences within and between organizations. In particular, such generalizations ignore the presence of subcultures (distinct affinity groups) within schools and IHEs, each of which is based on different cultural models, occupies different structural niches, and engages in different daily routines and practices. For instance, the identities, behavioral norms, and routines of administrators, teachers, and administrative support staff may vary substantially within one school or among different grade levels and disciplines. The tendency to ignore nuances has been discredited in sociology and anthropology for decades, largely because this "common-culture myth" fails to account for the fact that culture is continually evolving and varies within even the most homogeneous-appearing group. The view that a particular tribe or group has an unchanging and homogeneous culture oversimplifies cultural life, reducing members to mere carriers of culture X or culture Y. Furthermore, we know that culture in organizations is too complex to be explained by a single label or typology, largely because different groups and individuals will interpret public symbols, such as a school's motto or mission statement, in dramatically different ways (Becher & Trowler, 2003). Thus, it is unhelpful to talk about "the culture of K–12 schools" in general or "the culture of Central High School" in particular.

As noted in the introduction, it is more useful to think about organizations in terms of "cultural dynamics," which comprise the synergistic interactions among cultural models (norms and beliefs), structure and technologies, relationships, and routines and practices. Use of this cultural-dynamics approach will help you discern different groups' shared knowledge and behaviors within a single organization. In so doing, you will be able to account for the cultural diversity within schools and universities and build on (rather than ignore) the unique perspectives and life experiences that subgroups and individuals bring to the 3rd space of partnership.

## Focusing on Cultural Dynamics Within Organizations

The four cultural-dynamics elements (cultural models, structure and technologies, relationships, and routines and practices) typically coalesce around specific groups of people who share similar roles and responsibilities, which we refer to as affinity groups (e.g., an education-minded cohort of faculty within a physics department in an IHE). In particular, shared cultural models are found within specific affinity groups that share the same organizational niche, relationships, and daily routines. In this section, we focus on the importance of identifying and diagnosing cultural models, which are about the norms and beliefs governing a variety of topics, such as how to conduct a hiring process, interact with students, or collaborate with outside organizations.

We emphasize diagnosing cultural models instead of the structural features, relationships, and daily practices in which they are embedded because these facets of partner organizations probably will be dramatically altered or even absent within the 3rd space of partnership work. That is, new structures will be established, new relationships will be formed, and new practices will be required for partnership-related activities. However, cultural models tend to be both relatively immutable and highly portable, and probably will survive the transition from the home organization into the new partnership activity. This is not to say that understanding the other features of affinity groups is unimportant in developing a deep understanding of cultural dynamics. But conducting an organizational assessment or audit of each of these features is not feasible or desirable; you will need to focus your scarce resources strategically when engaging in pre-partnership planning. Thus, we recommend that you focus on cultural models, particularly the ones described, which our analysis of the UDEP project revealed to be especially important in partnership work.

### Your Own Assumptions and Mental Models

The first thing you should do is recognize yourself as a carrier of many different cultural models. Many of your thoughts, beliefs, and values have been internalized from your social and cultural environment, your upbringing, and your disciplinary or organizational affiliation. Gaining self-awareness is vitally important, because in a partnership setting, you probably will be interpreted and viewed in some fashion as a member of a particular organization or discipline. You also should identify the routine expertise you have acquired over years of experience in a school, an IHE, or another organization. This expertise evolved as responses to particular tasks and problems in these specific environments became routine or even predictable. Such skills and knowledge may include how to handle a challenging middle-school student, or teaching calculus to 19-year-old undergraduates. In each case, the knowledge is highly context specific. When you participate in a partnership, unless the focus of the work is your own organization (or classroom), you probably will not use your routine knowledge exactly as you have before. Instead, you will need to apply your expertise to a new situation or problem. Perhaps you will be faced with handling a challenging middle-school teacher in a professional-development workshop or teaching geometry to 12-year-old middle-school students. In any case, you will need to examine your own assumptions and mental models.

### Educational Hierarchies

One of the key types of cultural models to identify pertains to the educational hierarchies to which partner organizations belong. Hierarchical status differences are very important within the education profession, with an especially strong status distinction between professional roles both within and between the higher education and K–12 sectors. For instance, within higher education, full professors at research universities tend to be accorded the highest status, and fine gradations of ever lower status are made depending on the type and reputation of the institution and a person's rank within his or her institution. Researchers have noted that the cultural models that support the education profession's hierarchical nature are minefields for education partnerships (e.g., Sirotnik & Goodlad, 1988). These hierarchical distinctions become visible when people of markedly different status within each of these sectors interact and are very pronounced across the higher education/K–12 divide, but similar tensions exist elsewhere, too. Houck, Cohn, and Cohn (2004) write,

> The most important cultural dynamic is the assumption that universities have much to offer the schools, but that schools have little to bring to the relationship except a passive reception of delivered wisdom. A collaborative

relationship in which this assumption goes unexamined is likely to fail. (p. 36)

While it is easy for partnerships to be harmed by assumptions such as this, you can mitigate this danger by first acknowledging that these assumptions may exist in your particular situation, and then working to replace them with an ethic that all parties bring something valuable for solving the problem at hand. Failing to do so may hamper the development of a collective and synergistic working environment within a collaborative partnership, one in which every participant's voice must be respected if each person is to contribute effectively to the work. Within the UDEP partnership, the higher education leaders of the science professional-development group operated with the assumption that their K–12 district colleagues were their status equals. They went the extra mile, by listening respectfully and making clear to their K–12 colleagues that the standard hierarchical assumptions did not hold in this working group, and that the expertise of K–12 and IHE faculty was similarly valued and respected. They patiently worked on identifying their own and their K–12 partners' cultural models whenever they began to encounter resistance to the work or strong disagreements among the participants. Examples of relevant cultural models that members of the science professional-development group surfaced through intensive dialogue and a deepening sense of trust and openness include the following:

- Teachers, overwhelmed by the diversity of demands on their time, tend to protect themselves from new demands—a response that higher education staff sometimes interpret as inflexibility.
- Faculty will not understand the day-to-day realities of a K–12 classroom and will be more interested in "professing" to other participants than in participating as equals.

Because they identified these and other cultural models, the members of this group were better able to manage their frustrations, less likely to judge one another, and more likely to structure their work so it aligned with the practical limitations they all faced.

## Distinctions Between the Hard and Soft Sciences

Another well-known tension in education operates at the discipline level, with the hard sciences considered more rigorous and "scientific" and the soft sciences considered more speculative and less scientifically robust (Labaree,

2006). While this hard/soft disciplinary cultural model is most salient in higher education, it also operates within the K–12 sector, particularly at the secondary level, where teachers tend to work with others in their field, forming small groups or cliques comprising of disciplinary colleagues. Like the cultural models that place the higher education and K–12 sectors in hierarchical order, this hierarchical arranging of the sciences has a long history of derailing partnership efforts; these models are deep-seated and can lead people to respond with resentment and distrust with the smallest perceived slight.

Prior to the beginning of the UDEP project, I took the chair of one of the STEM departments to meet the director of our large education research center. The meeting was to discuss the possibility of advertising a joint position for someone with the disciplinary background in that science who in addition had exceptional experience and interest in learning. During the meeting, the STEM faculty could barely conceal his contempt for all things educational, and especially research. And the reaction was visceral—he said as we left, "Am I glad to be out of that building"—he was not remarking on the physical architecture!

(UDEP participant)

You should anticipate challenges of this type, pay close attention to encounters between these historically estranged groups, and create working environments that facilitate trusting and synergistic work.

## *Theories of Action*

A theory of action is a belief about the best way to address a problem and is one of the most important types of cultural models in partnerships. Underlying a theory of action is a deeper set of beliefs about how individuals and organizations change. For example, the belief that the best way to deliver professional development to K–12 teachers is through week long workshops followed by regular technical assistance meetings with curricular experts is a theory of action. In some cases, a theory of action may be held by just a few members of an organization, such as a handful of teachers in a given department who quietly take a different approach in their classrooms. In most cases, however, an organization's theory of action is visible in its policies and practices, is widely (and possibly unconsciously) held by members of the organization, and motivates decision making and how people go about their work. If your pre-partnership planning time is limited, focus on clarifying both your own and your potential partners' theories of action regarding the work or tasks at hand, because they will affect almost every aspect of your partnership.

> **Partnership Action Point:** A theory of action is a belief about the best way to address a problem. If you have time to identify only one cultural model of your partner, focus on their theory of action.

In the UDEP partnership, the partners thought they understood one another's theories of action for reforming math and science instruction in large urban school districts. However, it quickly became apparent that (at least) the members of the senior leadership group had failed to comprehend one another's approaches fully. After work commenced, misunderstandings about the role of higher education faculty and the nature of professional-development workshops for K–12 teachers became a flash point that undermined mutuality and trust. By contrast, the science professional-development group intentionally focused from the outset on identifying the theory of action of each partner group. In fact, over the course of the partnership, the group members developed a theory of action they believed was superior to the separate ones with which they began.

## *Technical and Adaptive Problems*

Are potential partners adept at dealing with technical and adaptive challenges in their daily work? Do they generally focus on the types of problems to which they can apply well-known solutions? These different stances became evident in the preservice math group, when both the mathematics and education faculty participants recognized that solving problems in their respective fields took very different approaches. In mathematics, problems have a clear and often narrow solution path, whereas in education, problems generally do not have clear solutions and often can and must be addressed in a variety of ways. These different cultural models manifested in the preservice math group not only in group members' approaches to mathematics problem solving but also in group members' approaches to general organizational problem solving. In other words, cultural models for technical and adaptive challenges can be strongly associated with disciplinary training, but they may also reflect a broader worldview.

## Partnerships and Collaborations

Potential partners' cultural models for how to engage with outside organizations are perhaps the most accurate predictors of how a partnership might unfold. Does a school or university typically engage in partnerships or other collaborative work? If so, what kinds of working arrangements is the organization accustomed to? Are they simple exchanges of resources, such as a K–12 district entering into a contractual arrangement with a private company for information technology training? In this case, an organization may be accustomed to limited partnerships, in which the organization interacts with partners as clients or customers and avoids collaborative work. Or is the organization accustomed to engaging in collaborative efforts that require collective decision making? If so, individuals in the organization might be skilled at working across organizational and cultural boundaries and engaging in participatory decision-making types of management. In partnership work, this cultural model will certainly affect the expectations and behaviors of partner organizations. Thus, it is useful to have some idea about each potential partner's cultural model for partnership and collaboration before engaging in the work.

## Evaluation and Assessment

Each organization has its own cultural models pertaining to how it monitors and evaluates itself. There may be self-study or strategic planning groups, regular audits of employee effectiveness, or no procedures at all. Additionally, different organizations may use evaluation information in different ways. Some may respond quickly, whereas others may change or evolve slowly, if at all. While it might not be useful to generalize about an entire organization based on its use of organization-wide assessment procedures, given that they may not reflect the procedures of a specific affinity group that will be involved in your partnership, you should pay attention to that organization's cultural models and practices regarding evaluation. Of particular importance is the degree to which a group or administrative unit is accustomed both to establishing procedures for evaluation and assessment and to demonstrating willingness to actively update and monitor the procedures. It is not uncommon for project participants to establish objectives and then to ignore them for the duration of the activities. Because this information is not going to be publicly available, you should ask your potential partners about their approach to evaluation and assessment and their track record for actively using data for reporting and program-improvement purposes. The key here is to ascertain whether your potential partners' cultural models for evaluation suggest a willingness to commit to collecting and using formative and summative evaluation data. Since assessment and accountability are critical features of partnerships and educational reform in the 21st century, discovering that an organization with a poor history of either or both should raise red flags.

## *Key Terminology*

Important cultural models that are central to specific disciplines or professions often are embedded in key terms. When these terms are unfamiliar to those outside the discipline, they stand out as puzzling jargon and require translation. These terms can cause confusion in partnerships. For example, "understand" and "explain" emerged in our study as terms that mathematicians and math educators used in very different ways. Mathematicians are trained to assume that an explanation should be very clear, include conventional notation, and be very detailed. In contrast, math educators generally use explanation to refer to the act of explaining and reasoning and to the notion that students should take up the practice of understanding the underlying concepts behind their problem solving. It is important to identify the discipline-specific cultural models carried by key terms, especially when the same term carries fundamentally different meanings for two groups.

## *Ethnicity, Gender, and Power Dynamics*

Besides cultural models related to educational work, each of us carries beliefs and values related to ethnicity, gender, and power dynamics. While you need not identify the different models each participant holds for these topics, they are a key part of individual and group identities and probably will affect your partnership work. In the UDEP project these models became evident in several instances. For example, some female participants in the senior leadership group and the preservice math group expressed the belief that some male IHE faculty showed more respect and deference for men than they did for women. While it may not be feasible to identify every cultural model involving ethnicity, gender, and power, be mindful that these models are potentially explosive.

## Agenda Items for Your Pre-Partnership Meetings

The following topics related to cultural dynamics and models should be considered in your pre-partnership planning meetings.

### *Key Cultural Models Salient to the Partnership at Hand*

One of the most important topics of discussion at a pre-partnership meeting is the cultural models that are likely to affect an educational partnership. This can be a difficult conversation to have, since cultural models are largely tacit, taken-for-granted systems of beliefs and knowledge that individuals have a hard time articulating. Begin with cultural models that are apparent to organizational members (e.g., a theory of action for improving science instruction) and engage a skilled facilitator who can cautiously draw out less apparent models. These issues should include educational hierarchies, theories of action, partnership and collaboration styles, evaluation and assessment, and key terminology. This last point is especially important, because it might otherwise never occur to some people that a particular term (e.g., "science inquiry," "explanation") may be interpreted differently by different people.

The Shasta Partnership, comprising leaders from the Shasta Union High School District; California State University, Chico; Shasta Community College; and the University of California Office of the President, successfully used this approach while attempting to improve college attendance in a mostly rural California county. The partners conducted a community cultural analysis using interviews, focus groups, and surveys of the partnering organizations and other stakeholder groups to identify each group's needs and characteristics. This type of information can be used not only to increase each partner's appreciation for the other partners' roles in the broader educational system but also to identify the key fault lines that separate groups from one another.

### *Ensuring Common Ground*

For a partnership to succeed, participants must have or reach a modicum of common ground on certain specific cultural models. Each organization may be interpreting the rationale for partnership in different ways, whether it is an internally motivated effort or a response to a request for proposals. In either case, it is critical to ensure that each group is interpreting the call to partnership similarly. In addition, the different organizations' theories of action must have some degree of overlap or commonality; otherwise there will be too much disjuncture or lack of fit between groups for them to have a common understanding of the best way to solve a problem. Once on some common ground, different groups can begin to assume that their partners are operating from a similar set of ideas and beliefs about a problem and its solution.

## Hidden Rules and Protocols

Each organization or affinity group will have what one participant called "hidden rules," which if violated may cause tension. For example, some groups may have protocols for designating recipients of e-mails. In the pre-service math group, some faculty insisted on not listing graduate students as primary recipients but relegated their names to the "cc" line. This angered many graduate students, who felt marginalized. While many people may not be able to articulate these hidden rules in a frank discussion of cultural differences, you should nonetheless pay close attention to your partners' practices and norms.

## Identify the Right Amount of Tension

By definition, partnerships bring together different groups and individuals, and it is inevitable that there will be some tension, especially in situations in which there are historic conflicts based on fundamentally different cultural models. Where these preexisting tensions or even outright hostilities are present, you should carefully assess whether there are sufficient prospects for finding common ground and developing the capacity to act in a coordinated manner. For example, our study revealed the existence of a particularly acrimonious history between a mathematics department and an education department at a research university and tension between the secondary and elementary science divisions within a K–12 district. The bases for these conflicts were a combination of mutually exclusive cultural models for things such as how to train K–12 teachers and relatively little interaction among the groups' members. In both cases, a small degree of common ground was created through partnership work, but the groups remained in many respects incompatible partners, and many participants expressed doubt that the effort was worth the outcome.

Some degree of tension, however, is a good thing, because partnerships are based on the premise of the whole being greater than the sum of its parts. Some differences cannot and should not be resolved but rather should be considered potential sites for learning and growth. Seely Brown et al. (2002) call this "creative abrasion," where ideas come into contact with one another productively instead of destructively (p. 76). For instance, in our study, the science professional-development group's initial meetings between STEM faculty and K–12 curriculum specialists were awkward, but the groups' members gradually developed a sense of appreciation for one another's skill sets and experiences. Thus, while partnerships need a certain amount of congruence, some differences should be appreciated because they constitute one of the primary benefits of a partnership arrangement. It will be up to you to discern which differences may provide opportunities for growth and learning (e.g., different areas of expertise) and which should be negotiated carefully or even avoided (e.g., differing views on education policy).

---

**Partnership Action Point:** In crafting new organizational structures and routines for a partnership, leaders can create an environment that facilitates the development of new cultural models.

---

The faulty idea of creating a new partnership "culture" is related to the problematic common-culture myth. Indeed, while we emphasize the importance of developing new affinity groups as a result of partnership work, the goal is not to knit together a common culture that all group members adopt but instead to find ways for different organizations to learn from one another and develop new capacities that could not be developed without the partnership. The notion that a partnership should create a new common culture sets up expectations that not only are unrealistic but also may inhibit the emergence of useful different cultural dynamics across different subgroups. That is, some subgroups from each partner organization may forge new 3rd-space identities—with some even developing into new affinity groups—whereas others largely maintain the cultural identities they came with.

### How Leaders Can Set in Motion the Creation of New Cultural Dynamics

Finally, although the argument that leaders can actively create, manage, and manipulate culture tends to be overstated, it is true that individual leaders play a major role in crafting the structure and routines of an organization, which in turn can influence the development of cultural models and educational practice. As Halverson (2003) argues, policies, curricula, and procedures can be potent tools to influence instructional behaviors in schools and universities, and this also holds true for partnership work. Leaders have the power to craft, at least in part, organizational structures and routines for participants in a partnership. They can design structural features to shape interactions and practice such that, over time, new routines and behaviors develop. If reinforced through repeated interactions and group acknowledgment of the collective nature of the work, new cultural models may emerge. A particularly important aspect of the organizational structure that can lead to the creation of new cultural models is the communications infrastructure, which we cover in detail in chapter 7.

## Chapter Summary

**Core Idea:** Viewing culture as a unitary and homogeneous set of beliefs or values—the common-culture myth—is neither appropriate nor useful for understanding partnerships. Instead, cultural models are widely shared knowledge and beliefs that accrue within specific affinity groups and are reinforced through structures, technologies, and routine tasks. Furthermore, cultural dynamics in partnerships should be thought of in terms of negotiating, not eliminating, the inevitable differences among groups. Through creative abrasion, these differences can produce new insights and innovations and should be encouraged.

### *Avoid the Common-Culture Myth*

- Be aware that the common-culture view masks subtle and important differences within organizations and groups.
- Attend to the broader contexts in which organizations function, such as tension between the soft and hard sciences.
- Identify the right amount of tension to support the kind of cross-organizational learning you want and that the partnership conditions will support.

### *Identify Specific Cultural Models*

- views about the educational hierarchy;
- theories of action related to the proposed work;
- tendency to work with technical or adaptive problems;
- collaboration and partnership;

- evaluation and assessment; and
- terminology and jargon.

## Agenda Items for Your Pre-Partnership Meetings

- Identify Key cultural models for each partner, especially their theory of action regarding the proposed work.
- Identify the "hidden rules" and protocols that guide each partner's professional practice.
- Consider how to foster new cultural dynamics by creating new routines and practices.

## Bibliographic Note

Almost every book and article on education partnership cites the importance of cultural dynamics, particularly in partnerships involving K–12 and IHE representatives. For particularly rich discussions of cultural dynamics in education partnerships, see Borthwick (2001); Kirschner, Dickinson, and Blosser (1996); and Sirotnik and Goodlad (1988). For research on cultural factors within IHEs, especially how institutional sagas and myths can shape people's identification with an institution, see B. R. Clark (1972). Clifford and Marcus (1986), DiMaggio (1997), and Martin (2002) each provide an introduction to the extensive literature on culture theory that argues against the common or unitary culture perspective. We are deeply influenced by work in cognitive anthropology, particularly recent work on cultural models that focuses on how individual cognition is related to group-level norms and belief systems. See D'Andrade (1995) for a history of this field and DiMaggio (1997) for an analysis of the relationship between cognitive psychology and culture theory.

For a review of the history of education schools and some of the tensions between education and other disciplines, see Labaree (2006). Research on disciplinary subcultures and distinctions in higher education includes that of Becher and Trowler (2003); for such research involving the K–12 sector, see Siskin (1991). For discussions of how to work with productive tensions and avoid trying to create a common culture in partnership work, see Parker and Selsky (2004) and Seely Brown et al. (2002). For an example of how culture influences interorganizational relations, see Wilkof, Brown, and Selsky (1995). Finally, for more information about the Shasta Partnership and other California-based pre-K–18 partnerships, see *Raising Student Achievement Through Effective Education Partnerships* by the California Alliance of Pre K–18 Partnerships (2004).

# 4

# CROSSING ORGANIZATIONAL
# AND CULTURAL BOUNDARIES

You cannot be a boundary crosser because you
decide to be one. You are a boundary crosser
because you invest the time that it takes to get
there.

(UDEP participant)

In management and organization science, the need to bridge the organizational and cultural boundaries that separate different groups has long been recognized as critical to successful intergroup relations. In education partnerships, the different groups include not only educational organizations but also different disciplines, government agencies, corporate partners, and parents and other community members. In arrangements comprising multiple organizations and types of constituencies, many people will need to talk to each other and share important information in a timely manner. This flow of information is largely accomplished by individuals known as "boundary crossers." Boundary crossers literally travel between different worlds, opening lines of communication, identifying and negotiating the different expectations people from different groups hold, and translating for the participating affinity groups the jargon that each uses. They are skilled at bridging differences, are empathetic and good listeners, and are aware of their own identities and biases.

Most important, boundary crossers establish effective and respectful communication and thus lay the groundwork for trust to develop among the partners. These individuals may be leaders who are in charge of designing and managing the partnership, or they may be project staff members who are on the ground interacting with many different stakeholder groups. Good boundary crossing is necessary in partnerships that seek to address complex technical problems. It is even more necessary if you are working on a complex adaptive problem, as innovative work is greatly enhanced by bringing together people from different areas of expertise. It is not easy to span boundaries, particularly when the issues are potentially controversial, such as how best to teach mathematics in middle school. In this chapter we discuss the importance of boundary crossing, key characteristics of individual boundary crossing, the process of boundary crossing, and ways to discuss these matters in your pre-partnership planning meetings.

## Why Boundary Crossing Is Important

Partnerships by definition comprise different organizations and constituencies. When they are brought together, boundaries will emerge that must be identified and negotiated. In this section, we describe the roles of boundary crossers and why they are important to smoothly run effective partnership operations.

### *Boundary Crossers Create Lines of Communication*

A boundary crosser acts as a conduit for information among disparate groups. This role is especially important during the beginning (i.e., forming and storming) stages of group development, because at this point, formal communication processes, such as regular meetings, are few, and familiarity and trust have not yet been established. After formal processes have been established and trust has developed, boundary crossers still play important roles, because they not only enhance formal lines of communication but also create personal ties and—as we describe below—dynamic, responsive links among groups. Furthermore, in complex, multiorganization partnerships in which information must trickle through multiple bureaucratic layers, the presence of boundary crossers at multiple points within the partnership helps improve communication and, if effective, lays the groundwork for building consensus.

### *Boundary Crossers Act as Culture Brokers*

Boundary crossers are culture brokers who acknowledge and value differences in the practices and cultural models of different groups. Thus, boundary crossers act as organizational anthropologists who observe and understand other groups on their own terms, and then help other participants identify and interpret the organizational and cultural boundaries that distinguish groups. Boundary crossers should not be expected to deal with all types of differences between groups; this would be an impossible task. Instead, they should focus on identifying specific relevant cultural models of the participating groups. We highlight a couple of these here. One cultural model of groups to which we assign primary importance is the theory of action that informs a group's proposed work. In chapter 3, we suggested that you learn each partner's theory of action during pre-partnership meetings. You also can learn about theories of action through your informal observations and by reading your potential partners' websites and publications. It is useful to be able to recall quickly, for use in real-time discussions and decision making, the significant ways in which these theories are similar to and different from each other.

Other types of cultural models that a boundary crosser should attend to are key terms and ideas that different groups may use but interpret differently. These terms, known as "boundary constructs," can serve as a point of contention or confusion between groups that are using the same words or phrases to mean different things. For example, the entire UDEP partnership used the term "science inquiry" in crafting the grant proposal, but different groups interpreted the term in different ways. Some viewed science inquiry as a one time professional-development workshop, whereas others considered it part of a comprehensive curriculum that school districts could adopt. This misunderstanding led to a disagreement among the partners that could have been avoided if a boundary crosser had identified the differences in how the groups used the term. Thus, boundary crossers need to address the meanings of boundary constructs for each group, and then help all participants either understand that different groups will have specific different interpretations of the terms, or create new, hybrid terms to which all parties agree.

## Boundary Crossers Incorporate Different Cultural Models in a Common Framework

Crossing boundaries also requires the skill and insight to position distinct cultural models and perspectives within a common framework. This does not entail merging different or disparate models, which might result in some models' or perspectives' losing out or being diminished through an unwelcome compromise. Rather, it involves identifying the different models as contributors to the overarching goals and objectives of the partnership, and inviting dialogue about how to deal with the differences. Indeed, in the nonprofit sector, where attaining a common or unitary culture between very different organizations is not only unlikely but undesirable, boundary cross-ers who can work effectively with different groups are increasingly valued. They were valued in the UDEP partnership as well. For example, a subcom-mittee of the preservice math group comprised representatives from a local K–12 district, education faculty and graduate students, and mathemati-cians. One of these individuals was a boundary crosser who had worked with most of these groups and thus had earned their respect and had a working knowledge of their daily activities and areas of expertise. Meetings this boundary crosser attended were usually more productive than ones he missed. Boundary crossers like this find common ground and frame prob-lems in ways that speak to the interests and characteristics of each group. In this way, they create a "collaborative mindset," identifying "connec-tions and possibilities where others might see barriers or limitations" (Lin-den, 2002, p. 167).

---

**Partnership Action Point:** Boundary crossers can begin to set the conditions for new, integrative cultural models to emerge. This requires understanding different models, and then creating work environments that facilitate coordination or collaboration.

---

Boundary-crossing work is important in setting the stage for effective partnership work. Creating work environments in which disparate views can be represented with respect and without fear of ridicule is a boundary cross-er's primary responsibility. With this cross-cultural framing in hand, bound-ary crossers must then foster excitement in all partners and motivate them to perform the partnership work with gusto. To do this, they must demon-strate that they understand and value each organization and its unique skills and needs.

## Characteristics of Boundary Crossing

In this section we review some of the key attributes of individual bound-ary crossers and the nature of the boundaries that typically separate organizations.

## Qualities of Individual Boundary Crossers

Boundary crossing requires particular skills and personality traits. Williams (2002) suggests that effective boundary crossers have the following traits, all of which involve effective communication:

- They are able to feel and listen with empathy and to build trust and familiarity.
- They are sensitive to and skilled in bridging the interests of individuals and organizations.
- They understand how to operate within formal organizational systems, while also being able to communicate over social landscapes.
- They are aware, or try to be aware, of their own biases and perspectives and of how these affect how they frame problems and interact with other people.

An effective boundary crosser is not trapped in his or her organizational or disciplinary identity, is able to think outside the box, and can speak the language of the "other" and compromise when necessary. By being aware that a person can activate an array of stereotypes and assumptions by the identity (e.g., professor, superintendent) or institutional affiliation of each, boundary crossers can defuse cross-group tension. Although not all individuals have the personality traits to be successful boundary crossers, certain boundary-crossing skills can be taught or learned. People who are not born boundary crossers, and who do not have the energy to develop effective boundary-crosser skills, should delegate tasks involving cross-organizational relations to others with the needed skills and traits.

Because the 3rd space of a partnership comprises multiple voices representing different organizations, a narrow perspective that fails to consider how a particular action ripples across the participating organizations can be problematic. According to Peter Senge (1994), a leading organizational scientist, a systems thinker is someone who can see how a collection of parts comprises a larger system and how changes in one part of a system can have effects on other parts. For instance, a typical high school comprises different subsystems such as the administration, discipline-specific departments, facilities, and a school board. A policy or staffing change in the administrative office may affect individual classrooms or staff, because each element is closely linked as part of a larger organizational system.

Because a partnership is often piggybacked onto existing organizational systems, a systems perspective should be applied not only to the partnership entity but also to each home organization. This is particularly important in reference to your own organization, so you can ensure that a partnership activity will not have deleterious effects on a subsystem within your own K–12 school or IHE. Thus, it is ideal if someone from your own organization who participates in the partnership is able to view organizations in these terms.

A systems approach also will inform how the problem the partnership is addressing is conceptualized. For instance, in the UDEP project, one leader felt that another leader's focus on the details of a series of professional-development workshops for K–12 teachers was "narrow thinking" that ignored the dynamic and systemic nature of education reform. In this case, the first leader felt that the workshops were being developed with little consideration of the broader science reform efforts within the district as a whole. He was certain that the coherence of the system would be compromised if the second leader changed summer workshops without consulting many other offices, and he suggested using path analysis or causal models to analyze the complex systems that underlie the different parts of district operations. The intent of this recommendation was to introduce a systems approach to understanding how K–12 districts function, which requires accounting not only for the microlevel of classrooms, but also for the macrolevel forces of school and district leadership, and district policies and politics. Although the second leader did not use the recommended path analysis, most of the leadership gradually accepted the need for systemic thinking in the partnership.

> Think of the partnership and your home organization in terms of interconnected subsystems, where changes in one can have positive or negative effects on the other.

## Multiple Boundaries to Cross

Recall that each organization in a partnership is distinguished not only by structural features such as organizational structures or hierarchical levels but also by deeply held cultural models that, for example, differentiate higher education from K–12 or the members of one academic discipline from another. If boundary crossing only required moving between clearly defined worlds, such as the world of workers and managers in a stereotypical industrial setting, leaders would only need to learn the language, routine tasks, and cultural models of one other group and would need to straddle only two cultural communities as they steered the organization. It is not that simple, however. Organizations comprise of multiple affinity groups, thus requiring boundary crossers to learn about several distinct groups (see Figure 4). In a typical high school, for example, these groups include teachers in different discipline-based departments (e.g., math, science, art), staff, administration, students in a variety of groups, and more. The diversity and complexity in a single education organization pose a considerable challenge to leaders in terms of boundary crossing.

Adding an entire other organization to the mix greatly increases the number of groups with which you must interact in a competent fashion. To complicate matters, it is likely that you lack in-depth knowledge about the other school or university and do not know to what degree groups that apparently correspond to those in your own organization are similar to or different from your own. For example, the UDEP project involved the mathematics departments of three different IHEs. One might assume that they would be similar because they all were in the business of teaching math

**FIGURE 4**
**Example of the intra- and interorganizational boundaries
that may require crossing in a partnership**

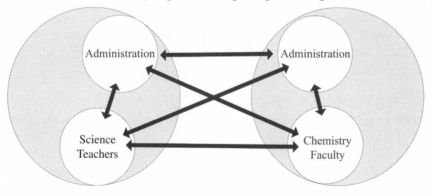

courses. However, they differed substantially because each had its own specific national and local identities, history, perspectives on pedagogical reform, and leader personalities. Moreover, within most named organizational units, such as mathematics departments, are subgroups, each with its own set of boundaries to identify and cross. For example, many math departments have subgroups that differ strongly from one another on the question of how to deal with mathematics courses for preservice teachers.

## *Multiple Boundary Crossers Will Be Needed in a Partnership*

No individual within a partnership should be placed in the role of "chief boundary crosser." In successful partnerships, leadership is distributed across many different people and organizational settings, with more leaders needed as the level of partner interdependence increases. Boundary crossers are needed at each point where disparate groups interact, from upper-level management to those on the ground planning the specific activities of the partnership. Thus, the more organizations in your partnership, the more boundaries there are to cross and negotiate. Having boundary crossers throughout the partnership greatly increases the odds that these boundaries will be negotiated in ways that generate buy-in from all participants. Having multiple boundary-crossing individuals is also an asset as the partnership work unfolds in the 3rd space. If left untended, boundaries can become fault lines for conflict and miscommunication. However, if negotiated successfully, they can become assets where different voices and areas of expertise can come together.

---

**Partnership Action Point:** Identify every point where disparate groups interact and try to place staff with boundary-crossing skills at these intersections.

---

In the UDEP partnership, the leader of the science professional-development group began her work by convening and facilitating groups of STEM faculty, education faculty, K–12 teachers, and administrators, each with its own distinct vocabulary and perspectives on science education. She created a work environment that encouraged respectful debate, where participants felt that their unique areas of expertise were valued. The group was also fortunate that a new member, who was especially skilled in boundary crossing, joined in the second year of the project and became a coleader of the group. Over time, the two leaders helped most of the almost 20 members of their group function as boundary crossers within subgroups of the group itself and for the home organizations to which each of them belonged. With this set of skilled boundary crossers, the group was able to "cocreate" high-quality professional-development curricula and professional-development processes for a large urban district. The science professional-development group exemplifies how, in partnerships, multiple boundary crossers are essential to efficient and effective organizational operations.

## Agenda Items for Your Pre-Partnership Planning Meetings

We recommend discussing the following topic related to boundary crossing in your pre-partnership planning meetings.

### *Leadership Qualities*

Again, while not all boundary crossers will necessarily be in leadership positions, it is ideal if the leaders of a partnership are adept at boundary crossing (or are willing to learn). These characteristics matter for leaders at all levels, from upper-level management to a small group facilitating a professional-development workshop. The presence at all levels of individuals with effective leadership styles and approaches will go a long way toward generating effective collaborative work.

### *Appreciation for Different Groups and Participants*

Good leaders show respect toward other affinity groups. Sirotnik and Good-lad (1988) hone in on a key quality: "One must be able to move readily back and forth between the culture of the school and the culture of the university, to have an understanding and appreciation of the values of both, and to be perceived as contemptuous of neither" (p. 220). Arrogance is a red flag. When working in partnerships, leaders ideally will be good listeners, respectful of other groups' ways of thinking and being, and able to speak in a jargon-free manner that appeals to all types of people. In our study, one of the most crucial leadership characteristics that participants noted was the ability to listen to other people's ideas. This ability allows leaders to negotiate not only school-university divides but also divisions among disciplines, personnel types (e.g., administrators, staff, and teachers), and many other different groups.

*Flexibility and Decision Making Across Boundaries*

Because change and evolution are defining characteristics of the 3rd space, leaders at all levels need to be willing to entertain alternative explanations and adjust their strategies. Such flexibility can be difficult even within one's home organization, and it can be doubly challenging when working with unfamiliar groups in an unpredictable environment. Do leaders in the various partner organizations have a record of flexibility, and do they seem to be able to change positions in the face of evidence? Do they have experience working in cross-organizational or interdisciplinary partnerships? If so, they probably have dealt with making difficult decisions or adjusting course in a complex organizational milieu. While lack of these traits and experiences should not be deal-breakers for your endeavor, the ability of project leaders and staff to exhibit flexibility is an asset to any partnership.

*Emotional Intelligence*

Finally, leadership is not a simple technical skill but instead requires a range of competencies. The trait of emotional intelligence is particularly useful in partnerships, given the certainty that leaders will encounter people from other backgrounds and training and that misunderstandings and conflict are likely to occur. Leaders with emotional intelligence are self-aware, can manage themselves and their emotions well, are socially aware of the people around them, and are skilled at managing relationships (Goleman, 1995). Guidance by leaders who are emotionally intelligent will increase the chances that the partnership will weather the inevitable storms and conflicts.

## Chapter Summary

> **Core Idea:** Cross-organizational relations require individuals known as boundary crossers who can establish communications and bridge differences between organizations and affinity groups, while also facilitating the development and maintenance of a common vision and goals.

*Boundary Crossers Are Important*

- They act as cultural brokers who can walk between worlds and translate the cultural models of one group for another.

- They open lines of communication among different individuals and organizations.
- They help to integrate different cultural models of various groups into a common framework that respects each group's differences while also fostering a common sense of purpose and identity.

## *Effective Boundary Crossing in Education Partnerships*

- Boundary crossers are not limited to leaders in your partnership and may be located at different levels of organizational hierarchies.
- Characteristics of effective boundary crossers include
  - They are good listeners, aware of their own biases, and skilled in working with diverse individuals and communities of practice.
  - They are systems thinkers who see the partnership in terms of interconnected parts, where an event in one part may influence other parts.
- Organizations have multiple boundaries to cross and a partnership exponentially increases the number of boundaries to deal with.
- By identifying boundary-crossing leaders at each major organizational boundary, and giving them responsibility for negotiating differences, a partnership is much more likely to turn cross-organizational and cross-affinity group tensions into productive and effective work.

## *What to Discuss in Your Pre-Partnership Planning Meeting*

- Discuss the importance of appreciating different communication styles, flexibility, and emotional intelligence for the leaders and project staff involved in partnership work.
- Consider the importance of boundary crossing at all levels of partnership.

## Bibliographic Note

There is extensive research on the role of boundary crossers or spanners in the organization and administrative sciences. For an early discussion of boundary crossing, see Aldrich and Herker (1977). Williams (2002) provides particularly valuable insights for education partnerships. While the education partnership literature does not deal at length with boundary crossing per se, the importance of fostering common visions and bridging differences is ubiquitous. See R. W. Clark (1988) for a discussion on the need to work across institutional and cultural differences to forge this common ground. Also consult Tsui and Law (2007) for a good review of boundary crossing and its implications for education partnerships, focusing on boundary crossing and learning in the case of university faculty, mentor teachers, and student teachers collaborating to develop new lessons. This study uses activity theory (see Cole & Engestrom, 1993) to study how different subjects use different mediating tools (e.g., technologies) while working together on a common task. For research on the importance of language in cross-organizational work, particularly the crucial role of boundary constructs, see Derry et al. (2000). Finally, for work on emotional intelligence, see Goleman (1995).

# PART TWO

## DESIGNING A PARTNERSHIP

I feel like we were building the train and sometimes we were thrown on the track and we were
getting run over by the train we were building.

(Administrator)

If as a result of your pre-planning meetings you have decided to establish a partnership, the information you obtained and relationships you began to develop during that period will serve you well in the next stage. This second stage, the design stage, also precedes actual on-the-ground work. In this part of the book, we consider different facets of partnership design. Perhaps the most important point about partnership design is that *no single type of partnership structure fits all circumstances*. Another key point is that while taking the time to design your partnership structure and administrative procedures up front will pay off during the implementation stage these structures and procedures probably will evolve over time.

Research in organizational science supports the idea that the 3rd space of partnership is unpredictable in nature. Ring and Van de Ven (1994) note that partnerships differ from traditional organizations, such as schools or universities, in that they are "socially contrived mechanisms for collective action that are continually shaped and re-structured by actions and symbolic interactions of the parties involved" (p. 96). New partnerships resemble start-up companies more than they do fully functioning organizations because they lack formal protocols for governance and known administrative units (e.g., departments). In addition, because they are not subject to the same organizational constraints, expectations, and procedures as are the partner organizations, leading a partnership requires the capacity to operate in an uncertain and emergent environment.

Important governance and power-sharing questions for the design stage include the following: What type of organizational structure (e.g., limited, coordinative, or collaborative) is needed? Is a new central administrative unit needed to oversee the partnership business? What are the power-sharing policies? What type of communications infrastructure should be established to facilitate effective and meaningful interactions among participants? Use a deliberative process to consider and answer each of these questions (particularly the one concerning the governance and power-sharing aspect of your partnership, because this can become a flash point that invites disagreement and conflict). Unfortunately, decisions about these critical organizational questions commonly are made by default or dictated by funders, with the players from each organization assuming that what works in their own organization will work in the 3rd space of partnership.

Take the time to consider the cultural models, organizational structures, relationships, and routines that each partner organization brings to the table. Then, taking into account these preexisting, and likely nonnegotiable factors, consider which administrative and governance arrangements are most appropriate for the particular tasks at hand. Your decisions should be guided by the nature of the tasks facing the group (e.g., are they long term and do they require multiple agencies?), the motivations of each partner (e.g., to maintain autonomy, to work interdependently), and the cultural compatibility of the groups. Determine ahead of time who has the authority to make decisions and what lines of authority should be followed. This is particularly important if the partnership involves organizations with leaders who are used to making unilateral decisions and not sharing or ceding authority. Take into account each partner's different organizational processes in areas such as communications, hiring, and work expectations, and knit a common framework for collective action. Use technology to create an efficient and highly productive communications system for your partnership, while not forgetting the continuing value of and need for face-to-face interactions and meetings.

If your partnership is tackling an adaptive challenge, you will need to be flexible and allow the working groups that are actually implementing the partnership to evolve over time. It might be advisable to adopt the philosophy of flexibility followed by the designers of the Condor distributed-computing project, a philosophy based on the following four elements:

- Let communities grow naturally.
- Leave the working groups in control, whatever the cost.
- Plan without being picky.
- Lend and borrow expertise and knowledge (Thain, Tannenbaum, & Livny, 2005).

The main point is to match the new partnership organization to the unique needs and constraints of your situation. Our analysis of the UDEP partnership and the research literature revealed that partnership leaders who started out focusing on implementation details at the expense of organizational process later realized that this approach cost them effectiveness and efficiency. Organizational structures and procedures that match the partnership's goals and objectives and each partner's organizational motivations are crucial because they create the administrative capacity to support the work and constitute the milieu for social cohesion and cultural dynamics.

# 5

# TYPES OF ORGANIZATIONAL STRUCTURES FOR PARTNERSHIP

Partnerships, contrary to popular myth, don't necessarily have similar organizations or require absolute collaboration and levels of equality among partners. In fact, partnerships can be organized in various ways, and collaboration can range from working together on specific activities to shared decision-making about all activities.

(Tushnet, 1993, p. 5)

In the introduction, we emphasized that there is no single correct partnership structure. Although we present in this book three types of organizational structures for partnership—limited or exchange partnerships, coordinated partnerships, and collaborative partnerships—in practice, any actual partnership will only approximate one of these types. These ideal types are models that are useful to consider during the design stage, when you are deciding which structure best suits your partnership. In this chapter we offer guidelines for selecting the best option to fit your situation. We offer guidelines for selecting the best option for your partnership.

There is no better use for all the information you gathered during your pre-planning meetings than for designing the type of organization that best suits the needs of your individual partners and your partnership as a whole. As we indicated in chapter 1, a key way in which partnerships differ is in the degree to which the partner organizations are interdependent. Tightly coupled partnerships (usually collaborative types) include joint ventures where partners are linked together by formal procedures and structures and may even include joint ownership. Loosely coupled partnerships (usually limited types) include consortia and associations, such as a trade association formed by firms to disseminate information and provide a platform for industry-wide education or lobbying. In contrast to tightly coupled structures, loosely coupled arrangements are less structured, more informal, and rarely entail joint action. Since relationships between individuals are a core aspect of partnership work, some scholars use the metaphor of familiar human relationships to understand partnership work (e.g., Teitel, 1998). We follow this convention to underscore the centrality of relationships to partnership efforts.

---

**Partnership Action Point:** Each partnership should be organized on its own terms. A partnership's structure may also evolve over time, in response to changing circumstances.

---

## Three Main Partnership Structures

Determining the organizational structure for your partnership is one of the most important decisions you will make. The structural configurations of your partnership will shape how people communicate and interact, establish routines, and develop new cultural models related to your particular effort. Adopting an organizational structure that suits your goals and objectives will increase the chance that your partnership will operate smoothly and efficiently, whereas a structure that is inappropriate may lead to the opposite result.

### *Limited Partnerships: Business Transactions*

Intriligator (1992) calls the most loosely coupled type of partnership a limited partnership. This type of partnership has a managing partner that maintains sole decision-making authority, with the other organizations providing services on a contract basis, similar to a consultant-client relationship (see Figure 5).

Relationships in limited partnerships are "strictly business" and not designed to enable group-based decisions or development of a new collective identity. In a limited partnership, the work is viewed as a service to deliver

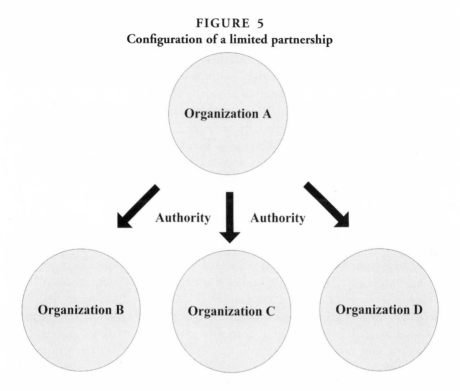

## FIGURE 5
### Configuration of a limited partnership

to a client or recipient group. A common example in education is IHE-based experts providing curriculum or professional-development materials to K–12 districts and schools. In these cases, the provider typically wields more power and influence than do the other participants. Although this type of organizational structure may reinforce the hierarchy of university expertise flowing downward, it nevertheless might be right for your partnership. For instance, it might be appropriate when one partner is only interested in delivering a product or service and not in engaging in any sort of collaborative activity. An organization that is motivated exclusively by self-interest might desire a limited role (as a client or as the sole managing partner), which can minimize negative effects on others while optimizing what the organization has to offer. The limited type of partnership is particularly suitable to situations in which one organization needs to maintain strong control of the nature of the work or in which an organization has a strong visionary leader with a singular and uncompromising vision of how to address the problem at hand.

Another term commonly used for limited partnerships is "networks," which comprise "constellations of businesses" arranged in a hub-and-spoke configuration, with a primary organization at the hub working with a diverse array of other organizations. A good example is Toyota's network, consisting of more than 180 first-tier firms that exchange parts or research outcomes with Toyota in return for funding and other resources. This structure allows Toyota to focus entirely on its core activity: designing and manufacturing automobiles. The benefits of this type of partnership are that each organization can focus on its own specialty area, and the arrangement is flexible, can operate with a quick product-development time frame, and can create a powerful competitive force (Barringer & Harrison, 2000).

### *Coordinated Partnerships: Friendships*

Organizations in a coordinated partnership are linked more closely than are those in a limited partnership, but they still enjoy a high degree of organizational autonomy. What distinguishes a coordinated partnership from the other types is that each organization agrees that it should bring to bear its different resources or strategies to achieve the partnership goals. They agree to coordinate their efforts through a loose governance structure that establishes the direction of the group but has little authority over the actions of each partner organization (see Figure 6).

In a coordinated partnership, each partner is responsible for its own piece of the pie and decides internally how to perform its tasks. In this sense, this type of partnership is like a friendship, as opposed to a business transaction. Other terms often used for the coordinated partnership type are "strategic alliance" and "consortium." These are often used when businesses coordinate their efforts to increase their marketing power in new regions or countries. In the context of education, a coordinated partnership may be formed, for example, among a city's high schools, local businesses, and community organizations to improve high school students' job-related skills

### FIGURE 6
#### Configuration of a coordinated partnership

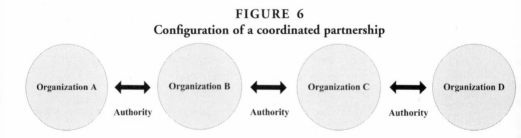

through workshops and other venues. The businesses commit resources because they need future workers, community organizations participate to increase job opportunities for their constituents, and schools participate because they believe the job-skills workshops will motivate their students.

## Collaborative Partnerships: Marriage

Many education partnerships strive to be what Intriligator (1982) calls a collaborative partnership. In a true collaborative partnership, the partners share a problem they believe can be addressed only if multiple organizations work together with a shared governance model. They not only appreciate one another's areas of expertise and trust one another but they also agree on the need for a high level of interdependence and collective governance, with decision making carried out by a central administrative unit (possibly an interagency board) (see Figure 7).

Collaborative partnerships work best in situations in which the participants recognize and honor the limits of their expertise and the value of others. This type of partnership is difficult to develop because partners must develop and sustain trust and respect even as they navigate the complexity and multiple tensions that come with a high level of interdependence. It is for these reasons that many authors liken collaborative partnerships to marriage—another type of union that carries both the promise of something better than each participant could achieve alone and the reality of tensions, misunderstandings, and disagreements that all too frequently result in divorce.

---

**Partnership Action Point:** Collaborative partnerships are both the most difficult and the most promising type of organizational arrangement.

---

"Joint ventures" are an especially tightly coupled subtype of collaborative partnerships. They are exemplified in education by professional-development schools, which are institutions created by K–12 districts and IHEs to focus on training K–12 teachers. Joint ventures are entities created by two or more firms that pool their resources to create an entirely separate, jointly controlled organization. A common reason for businesses to engage in joint ventures is to gain access to foreign markets. For example, a foreign supplier might form a joint venture with a local firm that has marketing skills, local

**FIGURE 7**
**Configuration of a collaborative partnership**

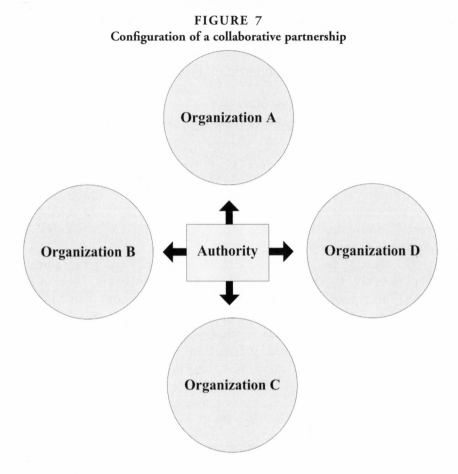

legitimacy, and relationships with customers. Joint ventures need high levels of managerial scrutiny and support and require significant planning for monitoring and governance. Although a joint venture involves two or more partners, it functions as an autonomous unit with a central administrative unit that has its own governance and leadership processes, and it often is overseen by a multiagency board of directors.

Collaborative partnerships are both the most difficult and the most promising type of partnership. If you choose to design a collaborative partnership, your challenges are not limited to hammering out a shared administrative structure that is enabled by participatory decision making and shared governance processes. You also must use effective boundary-crossing practices, communicating among partners vertically and horizontally and in line with the partners' various cultural models, to develop the needed trust and common understandings. In the absence of a top-down decision-making governance design, trust among groups is particularly important to weather the challenges of jointly addressing problems, many of which will be unexpected. What makes this type of partnership all the more challenging is that collaborative decision making and boundary crossing are skills that are difficult to learn, develop within education institutions haphazardly, and must be learned by individuals at all levels of the partnership (Owens, 2001). That said, a truly effective collaborative partnership can be transformative and leverage various groups' assets and expertise to address complex educational problems.

## Selecting a Partnership Type

Education partnerships are complex and multifaceted enterprises that challenge even the most adept planners. In the business world more than 50% of partnerships fail, so attention to design is crucial. Designing effective cross-organizational partnerships is akin to crafting an entire organization from scratch and without a template. Many leaders say that some of their most challenging experiences with partnerships take place during this stage. All too often, groups find each other's boundaries only when they run into them and figure out after painful mistakes, costly inefficiencies, and stressful misunderstandings occur that they need more effective structures and procedures. Early encounters of this type exacerbate the inherent tensions in partnership work, just when lines of mutual trust are likely to be the weakest. One reason for this pattern is that while leaders generally pay plenty of attention to the content of the work (e.g., how to design summer professional-development workshops, how to improve teaching) they pay too little attention to the cross-organizational structures and processes they need to enable that work. Only by giving this design stage sufficient time and attention will you be able to create the administrative capacity you need to achieve your goals.

As we've stated before, there is no one-size-fits-all organizational structure for partnerships: the diverse needs and conditions of each partnership make a universal organizational structure unworkable (Tushnet, 1993). Although each partnership needs to tailor its structure to its own needs, certain general principles can help you choose appropriate interorganizational structures and processes. These principles can be summarized in one statement: the organizational structure and processes should match the nature of your partnership's goals and objectives and the partners' motivations, capacities, levels of desired interdependence, and cultural compatibility. Much of the information about these factors will be at hand if you have conducted effective pre-partnership meetings, as described in part one of this book.

---

**Partnership Action Point:** The organizational structure and processes should match the nature of your partnership's goals and objectives and the partners' motivations, capacities, levels of desired interdependence, and cultural compatibility.

---

## *Factors to Consider When Selecting an Appropriate Structure*

The different factors you need to consider when making decisions about the appropriate organizational structure for your partnership are summarized in Table 2, which indicates how each factor appears in different partnership types. Use this table to guide your thinking about the organizational type best suited for your partnership. No single factor should dictate your selection of a partnership structure; the decision should take into account the full set of factors. For this analysis, we draw heavily on Intriligator's excellent 1992 recommendations for selecting partnership structures.

### *Nature of the Problem*

A technical problem is one that experts know how to identify, define, and solve. An example of a technical problem is how to fly an airplane. In contrast, an adaptive problem is one that even experts have not clearly defined or solved, such as how to deal with climate change. Your decisions about which organizational structure to adopt should be informed by the degree to which your problem is technical or adaptive. When a partnership is addressing a strictly technical problem, a limited partnership makes sense because the problem and its solution, however complex, are understood, and procedures and roles are worked out. Hence, hierarchical systems are needed to implement a more tightly coupled organizational structure and protect the organization from disruption by outsiders who might cause staff to be distracted from the work at hand or seek to redirect the organization's resources.

**TABLE 2**
**Characteristics of the three different partnership types**

| | *Limited* | *Coordinated* | *Collaborative* |
|---|---|---|---|
| **Nature of the Problem** (i.e., technical or adaptive) | Technical problem (routine and focused with well-known solution) | Mix of both technical and adaptive problems | Adaptive problem (novel and lacking well-known solutions) |
| **Goals and Objectives** | | | |
| Time Required | Short term | Intermediate or long term | Long term |
| Number of Partners Required | A few | A few or several | Several |
| **Motivations** | Primarily self-interest | Combination | Enlightened self-interest (i.e., self and the broader collective) |
| **Capacity and Resources** | Limited | Medium | Substantial |
| **Autonomy** (desired level) | High | Medium | Low |
| **Cultural Tensions** (level of) | Likely to be slight | Likely to be moderate | Likely to be severe |

In contrast, when a partnership is addressing an emergent challenge, there is no set of defined procedures to implement, and efficient, hierarchical organizational structures are likely to be damaging rather than useful. What is needed is a more flat and open organizational structure, in which nonauthoritarian boundary crossers can mobilize the engagement of people who possess the different viewpoints and expertise needed to help the partnership understand the problem and to design promising objectives and strategies. Rather than structures that protect staff from disruption by outsiders, the structures should foster the kind of trust building and creative abrasion among diverse players needed to solve the problem. The nature of the problem that most partnerships identify lies somewhere between the two extremes of a strictly technical problem and a fully emergent challenge. It is important therefore to consider, and agree upon, where on this continuum your problem lies.

*Goals and Objectives*

As we have seen, the nature of your goals and objectives is key factor to consider when choosing the type of organizational structure most appropriate for your partnership. Consider the amount of time needed to achieve the goals and the number of partners involved. The longer the time, the more emergent the problem to be tackled, the greater the number of partners (and the more interdependent the partners' roles), the more collaborative the organizational structure needs to be, and the stronger the role of a central administrative group. Conversely, if you determine that your goals are short term and require only one or two agencies, perhaps a more limited partnership is more appropriate.

*Motivations*

Each organization's rationale for engaging in partnership provides a strong indicator of the organizational structure that will best suit the partnership. For instance, if each partner is motivated by enlightened self-interest and the welfare of the entire partnership and community is a priority, a collaborative partnership is appropriate. On the other hand, if you sense that one partner is motivated by opportunism more than by the desire for a true partnership, then a more limited structure—in which the more self-interested organization serves as a subcontractor or the primary partner—will minimize the potentially negative effects on others of that organization's involvement while benefiting from the assets it may bring to the table. This type of partnership implies a governance model that is completely autonomous and limited to a single organization.

*Capacity and Resources*

An organization's material, human, and social capacities also should be considered when making decisions about your partnership structure. One aspect of capacity to take into account is the turnover rate of leadership, which, if high, can affect an organization's ability to follow through on its commitments. If an organization is experiencing high turnover, its capacity should be considered relatively low, or at least unstable, which argues against the organization's becoming too tightly coupled in a collaborative partnership. However, these decisions must be made on a case-by-case basis, as a high-turnover organization nevertheless may be sufficiently committed.

Another critical issue to consider is the level of resources available from the funding agency or other supporters. If inadequate resources are available to implement the partnership activities, then you should strongly consider using the limited partnership–type structure, which requires the least amount of time, energy, and resources to manage. But even if you have enough resources to fund your partnership, a collaborative partnership is not automatically the best vehicle; your decision should take into account the other factors as well. Finally, a sometimes overlooked aspect of capacity is geographic distance. If your potential partners are geographically dispersed, then you will need additional resources (e.g., travel, communications technology) to coordinate activities effectively. You should scrutinize this factor closely if you are considering a collaborative partnership, because regularly bringing together people from far-flung locations is expensive and challenging.

### Autonomy and Interdependence

If a high degree of interdependence (and thus, low autonomy) is desired by all partners and deemed necessary to achieve your goals, a collaborative partnership may be the most appropriate organizational structure. In contrast, if a partner is unable or unwilling to participate in joint decision making and scrutiny, a collaborative partnership is not a wise choice. For many K–12 schools, IHEs, and other organizations, the time and energy required to participate effectively in a highly interdependent partnership may not be available. If this is the case, a limited or coordinated partnership may be the best vehicle for achieving the partnership's goals.

### Cultural Tensions

Cultural tensions among education organizations and disciplines are inevitable regardless of the type of partnership structure. Thus, you need to assess your ability and willingness to tolerate the level of tension that seems likely. Generally speaking, if the tensions are severe, you should avoid a collaborative structure. When assessing the likelihood of tension, it is especially important to consider the following factors:

- the gap between partners' cultural models for the educational hierarchy, the soft/hard science divide, and other key cultural models discussed in chapter 3;
- the degree of alignment of the partners' theories of actions (and if you are externally funded the funder's theory of action);
- the extent of the differences in leadership styles of key leaders in each partner organization; and
- the compatibility of the key leaders' personalities and whether these individuals are positively or negatively embedded in other communities or relationships.

Based on these considerations, you should be able to discern whether the level of cultural tensions in your partnership will be severe, moderate, or slight, which will then suggest a particular type of partnership structure.

## Making the Decision About Partnership Type

After analyzing each of these factors, you should be able to determine the most appropriate partnership type for achieving your goals and objectives. Once the partnership type has been selected, the decision should be communicated clearly to all stakeholders involved so everyone has clear and accurate expectations about their own roles and responsibilities (Tushnet, 1993). The next step is to design administrative and leadership protocols to implement and manage your partnership.

## Chapter Summary

---

**Core Idea:** There is no single type of organizational structure for partnerships. The organizational structure and processes should match the nature of your partnership's goals and objectives, motivations, organizational capacity, level of desired interdependence, and partners' cultural compatibility. Do not assume that a collaborative partnership is the best option, because, while this type of partnership holds great promise, it is also the most difficult to design, implement, and manage.

---

### The Three Main Partnership Types

- In limited partnerships, the most loosely coupled organizational structure, one managing partner interacts with others solely on a subcontract or client basis. This partnership type includes service-delivery partnerships, in which one organization provides services to another.
- In a coordinated partnership, organizations work together with a loose governance structure, no single organization is in charge, and responsibilities and tasks are not centrally coordinated. Each organization concentrates on its own "piece of the pie" while working toward the partnership's common goal.
- In collaborative partnerships, the tightly coupled model, different organizations share a common goal and set of responsibilities, and all

activities are closely coordinated. This type of partnership requires organizations to share decision making and to develop a shared sense of obligation to the collective.

## *Factors to Consider When Selecting an Appropriate Organizational Structure*

- *Nature of the problem:* A technical challenge may not require a high degree of collaboration and interdependence, while an adaptive challenge (i.e., one that demands flexibility and innovation) probably would suffer under a top-down organizational structure.
- *Goals and objectives:* The time required to achieve your goals and the number of partners involved might indicate a particular type of structure. Generally speaking, the more complex and involved the task at hand, the more likely a collaborative partnership is appropriate.
- *Motivations:* Consider the degree of self-interest of organizations in the partnership. The more an organization is focused on its own self-interest instead of on the well-being of the collective, the less appropriate a collaborative partnership will be.
- *Capacity:* Organizations that possess high material, social, and human capacities will be more capable of participating in a collaborative partnership, whereas those with limited capacities will be less capable.
- *Autonomy and interdependence:* If an organization wants to maintain high levels of autonomy, a limited partnership is desirable.
- *Cultural tensions:* If there are likely to be severe cultural tensions among different groups, a collaborative partnership might be untenable and ripe for conflict.
- *Leadership:* The capability of leaders to commit their time and resources fully to a partnership effort, as well as their abilities to cross organizational and cultural boundaries, should also be taken into consideration.

## Bibliographic Note

For a discussion of how to select organizational types for partnerships, see Barbara Intriligator's excellent 1992 analysis in *Establishing Interorganizational Structures That Facilitate Successful School Partnerships*. Intriligator's work is one of the most specific regarding how to select organizational structures for partnership work. Tushnet's 1993 guide to developing partnerships also provides valuable information about creating appropriate organizational structures. For insights about best practices in selecting organizational models in a series of California-based education partnerships, see *Raising Student Achievement Through Effective Education Partnerships* by the California Alliance of Pre K–18 Partnerships (2004). For analyses of professional-development schools, perhaps the best known types of partnerships in education, see Sirotnik and Goodlad (1988).

For a discussion of different types of partnership structures, see Barringer and Harrison (2000), Gray (1989), Linden (2002), Waschak and Kingsley (2006), and Whetten (1981). For a discussion of the role of trust in collaborative work, the subject of chapter 10, see Mohr and Spekman (1994) and Vangen and Huxham (2003). For analysis of challenges associated with collaborative work in education, see Owens (2001).

# 6

# ADMINISTRATION AND LEADERSHIP

In 1985, the University of Washington's School of Education and nine school districts formed the Puget Sound Educational Consortium to coordinate on school renewal efforts in the region. At first the consortia was governed by a Coordinating Council that had equal representation from each partner, and made decisions based on consensus and information provided from task forces. However, a newly hired executive director had a more top-down managerial style and an agenda for teacher leadership, which was implemented without formal approval by the Council. Predictably, problems ensued regarding the appropriate organizational structure, management style, and agenda setting for the Consortia.

(Keating & Clark, 1988)

As we have noted, administrative structures and processes are more difficult to establish and enforce in the 3rd space of partnership than they are in individual organizations (Thomson & Perry, 2006). This is because partnerships (1) function across system boundaries and without well-thought-out policies and procedures to support collective action across these boundaries, and (2) routinely face unpredictable challenges and novel situations. Further complicating the administration of partnerships is the need to integrate the different expectations that various professional communities have for how organizations should be administered, how leaders should lead, and how decisions should be made. For example, referring to governance, fiscal management, and intellectual property policies, one administrator in our study noted that two of the universities involved "are just totally different institutions in terms of the way they look at the world."

---

**Partnership Action Point:** Look for leaders with adaptive expertise—the ability to craft solutions in unpredictable environments, make decisions while coping with ambiguity, and "build the airplane while flying it."

---

Because partnership work probably will implicate these and many other organizational policies and practices, in the first part of this chapter we focus on helping you to identify relevant administrative procedures of each partner organization to assess whether these are well suited to your partnership work, and how to proceed if they are not. In the second part of the chapter, we discuss choosing and supporting the leaders who will craft and implement your partnership's administrative procedures and policies. These are the people who will coordinate the day-to-day operations of your initiative and engage in troubleshooting. You need leaders who can fulfill these responsibilities in a manner that suits your particular partnership. Look for leaders with adaptive expertise—the ability to craft solutions in unpredictable environments, make decisions while coping with ambiguity, and "build the airplane while flying it." In the third part of the chapter, we identify two other related topics that deserve special attention: financial management and evaluation.

## Governance

Governance refers to the processes, customs, and policies affecting the way an organization is directed, administered, or controlled. Embedded in these processes and policies are decisions about how decision making and other responsibilities are distributed among organizational roles or positions. Decisions about governance will greatly affect how your partnership operates and what it is able to produce. The relationships between general governance systems and partnership types are summarized in Table 3.

For instance, if you are in a limited partnership, then a top-down approach may be reasonable. This is particularly true if the problem at hand

**TABLE 3**
**Relationship between partnership and governance types**

| Partnership Type | Governance Type |
|---|---|
| Limited | Top-down |
| Coordinative | Shared |
| Collaborative | Shared/consensus-based |

is a technical challenge. However, if you have an adaptive challenge, then a more consensus-based decision-making approach may be more appropriate. This pairing of partnership and governance type is just a starting point for discussion about governance within your group. Think of the top-down and shared governance models as two ends of a continuum and, taking into account your partnership's characteristics, decide where on this continuum your partnership fits best.

## *Principles of Governance in Partnership*

You should keep in mind three principles as you consider governance topics. The first is that when making decisions about partnership governance, it is important to take into account the prevailing cultural models related to governance of your partner organizations. Some of the decisions your partnership makes might need to be reviewed by the home organization—a school board, a department, or an internal leadership group. For example, Henry Mintzberg et al. (1996) tell of a Canadian consumer goods company that was exploring a new line of eco-friendly products with the assistance of an environmental group. The company insisted on holding private discussions to ensure that it would be the first to market the products. The leader from the environmental group agreed; however, he faced a revolt in his own organization, in which consensus-based decision making was highly valued, and he was forced to resign. Mintzberg et al. argue that "back-home commitment building" is a key facet of partnership, and that incompatibility between governance systems does not bode well for successful initiatives (p. 6). Thus, a partnership with a governance system that is poorly aligned with the systems of the home organizations, especially the organizations where on-the-ground partnership activities are taking place, may find it difficult to have its decisions accepted and institutionalized.

**Partnership Action Point:** When making decisions about partnership governance, it is important to take into account the prevailing cultural models related to governance at your partner organizations.

The second principle is that change—in personnel, events, and circumstances—will probably be a constant presence in your partnership, so the governance system you initially establish probably will require modification. This is particularly true at the beginning stages, and as Sirotnik and Goodlad (1988) observed more than 20 years ago, "How best to govern and administer collaborations that are still in an amorphous, developing stage should continue to remain an open question" (p. 221). One variable to which you should pay special attention is the emergence of particularly strong or weak leaders whose characteristics may or may not fit the governance system well. Changes within partner organizations, such as budget crises or staff turnover, or internal developments in the partnership itself, may also necessitate revising your decision-making procedure. The key point is to be prepared to modify your administrative procedures to best fit the situation.

The third principle is that trust and partnership loyalty play critical roles in governance. If there is no trust among partner organizations, or among key leaders who represent partner groups, it will be very difficult to make sound decisions and implement them. Trust is needed in limited partnerships that use top-down governance models; even the most formal contractual arrangements must be honored for a limited partnership to succeed. Trust and loyalty within the partnership are far more significant factors in a collaborative partnership using a consensus-based governance model. They motivate members of on-the-ground working groups to take on challenging tasks, motivate leaders to make decisions that optimize the partnership resources in ways that benefit both home organizations and the collective, and motivate technical and fiscal support staff to go out of their way on behalf of the partnership, for example, by providing an extra bit of information or staying late to meet a deadline.

### Attributes of Top-Down and Shared Governance Models

Governance in education organizations can be organized into two idealized models: top-down governance and shared governance.

## Top-Down Governance

Many organizations have top-down, hierarchical governance systems in which chief executive officers (CEOs) and other leaders make unilateral decisions. Many districts and schools, and some IHEs are run in a predominantly top-down fashion. These organizations use a governance model where many decisions are made by leaders at the top of the hierarchy. For instance, while operating within the constraints of federal- and state-level policies and procedures, superintendents and principals in many K–12 districts and schools have decision-making authority over many functions of their organizations. The organizational structure used with this governance model takes the form of a pyramid, with leaders at the top, workers at the bottom, and authority flowing downward. This structure is efficient and effective when the organization has well-defined procedures and tasks and the leaders are knowledgeable, consistent, and fair in exercising their authority. If your partnership chooses to operate with a top-down governance model, it is important to clarify that there is just one top position and to articulate the amount of authority that devolves to positions below the top. Then it is crucial to make clear which individuals hold the top role and which hold any subordinate leadership roles. If individuals who are accustomed to holding top-level authority in their home organization agree to play a subordinate role in the 3rd space of a partnership, they must monitor their behavior carefully. Any slip into executive decision-making behavior on their part is likely to be viewed as an unfriendly, insubordinate act.

## Shared Governance

Generally speaking, IHEs use a shared governance system. Individuals holding top-level positions (e.g., chancellors, presidents, and provosts) may have some top-down decision-making authority, but they usually use it sparingly, relying for the most part on the power of tradition and on the influence associated with their position to shape organizational directions and policies. Stories abound of university leaders' authoritative decisions being met with faculty revolt. Within colleges and universities, everyday policy-making authority usually devolves to individual colleges or departments, and sometimes even to individual faculty. A shared governance system is often cited as a key ingredient for successful education partnerships, because it is viewed as an essential element for fostering trust, familiarity, and collective ownership of the initiative throughout and within the partner organizations (e.g.,

Sirotnik & Goodlad, 1988). In a partnership, shared governance usually consists of representatives from each organization coming together in a consensus-based decision-making body in which all partners collectively make decisions about the group's key functions. These may include decisions about resource allocation, program management and implementation, and stakeholder engagement. The centrality of this participatory element of shared governance led Naida Tushnet (1993) to use the term "distributed leadership" (p. 28) to describe this approach to partnership governance.

---

**Partnership Action Point:** In a shared governance model, emphasize participative decision-making processes and minimize hierarchical and top-down authoritative structures.

---

Such an approach is not without its challenges. One challenge in developing a shared governance model is ensuring that the governing body represents the stakeholder groups. One guideline for ensuring adequate representation is to invite to the decision-making table one representative from each of the partners or stakeholders that ultimately must play a significant role in the initiative. All participants must be accorded an equal say in partnership-related decisions. Barbara Gray (1989) notes that if collaborative partnerships using shared governance, are to achieve outcomes that reflect group consensus and not coalition or power politics, a participative decision-making process should be enacted, hierarchical and top-down authoritative structures should be minimized, and all partners must be willing to accept that each organization has interests. This last point is particularly important because there must be a willingness to acknowledge that all participants have legitimate concerns and equal voices. Without this mutual respect and willingness to cede decision-making authority to representatives of all partners, the arrangement probably will become a top-down governance system with a particularly powerful individual or clique calling the shots. This is a key reason why researchers counsel against jumping into a partnership without first considering these issues, particularly if a school or university has little or no experience with consensus-based governance.

### Key Governance Topics to Consider

Decisions about your partnership governance model will entail the often touchy issues of organizational autonomy and power dynamics. Your group must engage in activities that many people find uncomfortable, such as clarifying each partner's role in the enterprise, determining who is eligible to make decisions and about what topics, deciding what actions are allowed or constrained, and deciding how much information about what topics needs to be shared with which partners. To be truly effective, these decisions about decision making must be collectively understood, agreed on, and willingly complied with.

Key elements in the process of formulating a governance model for your partnership are described next.

*Authority in the Partnership: Who Is Empowered to Make Which Types of Decisions?*

It is vital to determine where decision-making authority will reside in your partnership. Will there be a central body making crucial decisions, such as the UDEP's senior leadership group, or will there be a single individual who has a stronger leadership role within the collective? Will this decision-making body be constituted of top-level managers, on-the-ground project staff, or both? Once you determine who is empowered to make decisions, you must decide what they will be allowed to make decisions about. Will a central governing group make all fiscal decisions, or will specified amounts of funding be allocated to each partner, which then makes its own spending decisions? Can the decision makers determine the specific activities of the partnership (e.g., developing a new math professional-development workshop), or should those decisions be left to project staff?

Then you must establish policies and procedures for selecting who will play these roles, and for guiding these decision makers when they are exercising their authority. Will they be allowed to act only with the approval of an advisory board, or will they have autonomy? Will decisions be made in regular monthly meetings or on an as-needed basis? Perhaps most important, how will you handle dissent? Are decisions to be made by a majority vote, or will a consensus be required? Strong disagreements will occasionally occur, so you should have in place a mechanism such as a "majority rules" provision or a dispute mediation process.

---

**Partnership Action Point:** Discuss precisely what sort of entity is empowered to make decisions in your partnership, what the entity has authority over, and what procedures guide the decision-making process.

A special challenge endemic to many policy-inspired partnerships is that the governance structure is determined in effect by the policy maker/funder. For instance, most federally funded partnership grants require that a principal investigator be appointed or hired; this person is responsible to the granting agency for the competent administration of the project. If your project comes with a formal leadership role such as this, you should discuss with your partners the implications for the partnership. If you are attempting to use a collaborative partnership structure, should you agree that this person will not have the authority to act without the consensus of the group, and that if he or she does, those decisions can be overridden? And if you agree on this policy, how will you convey this decision to the funding agency?

*Boundaries: What Actions Are Allowed or Constrained?*

You should also determine what types of actions the partnership can engage in and specify sanctions for noncompliance and processes for identifying noncompliance and implementing the sanctions. This rule setting demarcates for all participants the boundaries of the decision-making body's authority. For instance, if a school makes it clear that a partnership working on elementary science curricula will have no authority over the school's eighth-grade classes, then the people in the partnership will understand the limits and scope of their actions. This measure will help ensure that home organization autonomy is maintained and respected. Efforts to clarify boundaries are only effective if the partners are willing to monitor themselves, comply with the established rules, and implement the identified sanctions for noncompliance.

*Embedded Relationships Among the Partner Organizations*

Related to boundaries is the issue of embedded relationships. It is important to acknowledge the kinds of preexisting or embedded relationships that your partners have with other organizations or individuals who are relevant to the partnership. It may be necessary to determine whether and how these relationships will be integrated into the partnership, or if they are considered "off limits." For instance, in UDEP, one of the university partners had preexisting relationships with several K–12 districts. These partners felt it was very important that the work they had done to develop these relationships not be impaired as a result of their participation in the new partnership, so clear barriers needed to be drawn around the embedded relationships.

## Information Policies and Procedures

Effective information sharing enables groups and individuals within a partnership to complete tasks efficiently, builds trust and satisfaction, and often leads to new ideas and new exchanges of valuable information (Perkins, 2003). To achieve these outcomes, the partner organizations need to agree on which types of information they will be expected to share, what types of decisions will be communicated to whom, and how. These decisions should be closely linked to the type of partnership structure you select. For example, in a limited partnership, only a select few individuals or groups will need to be in the loop. This approach is characterized by the high value of efficiency, where information is provided on a need-to-know basis only for those people who are essential to get the work done.

In a collaborative partnership, there probably will not be many a priori limits on information sharing. To achieve the benefits of a true collaboration, you should foster an atmosphere of openness and trust so you and your partners will feel that your own organizational interests will not be harmed, but instead will be advanced, by sharing important information. For example, news of the impending resignation of a superintendent should be shared so the potentially affected working groups can make necessary adjustments. There are, however, limits to what information needs to be shared. Sharing nonessential information should be minimized. We recommend that you begin a collaborative partnership with relatively few limits on information sharing and add limits as partners begin to experience information overload. Whatever your information policies are, however, make them explicit and easy to find and share them with new members.

## Governance at Different Levels of the Partnership

In K–12 schools and IHEs, different groups are responsible for governance at different organizational levels (e.g., campus-wide, college or department level, center level, course level) and for different types of organizational activities (e.g., personnel, buildings and maintenance, legal affairs). Each of these groups within a particular institution may operate with a different governance model. In partnerships, it might be necessary to establish a similarly diverse set of governing styles across different groups, based on their unique needs and conditions. Decision-making authority should not be limited to senior leaders and managers but should be granted to leaders at all levels, with plenty of responsibility held by the working groups on the ground. This will enable the working groups to function more effectively.

## Selecting Leaders

Selecting leaders is one of the most important aspects of designing a partnership. You should consider the following three factors when choosing your partnership's leaders: leadership styles, leaders' professional allegiances, and the importance of fostering distributed leadership. Additionally, partnership leaders must pay attention to social coordination, that is, effectively communicating to a diverse range of participants the jointly determined rules and procedures that govern the partnership. Typically this role falls to a leader who is an effective boundary crosser, who can work out the inevitable kinks in the administration of the partnership while also improving the exchange of information and ideas among the diverse partners. Thus, a critical decision in your partnership is to choose a leader who can cross organizational and cultural boundaries and oversee the partnership's administration and decision-making apparatus.

### *Leadership Styles*

Leadership styles should be matched to the partnership structure. For instance, an effective leader for a limited partnership may be someone who is accustomed to having executive control of an organization and has demonstrated the capacity for success in a vertical power structure, rather than someone who prefers to draw consensus-based decisions out of a diverse group of colleagues. On the other hand, in a collaborative partnership, the most effective leaders will be people who understand how to work with different people and can span organizational and cultural boundaries to find a common ground for collective action. Be aware that some leaders simply cannot work together as a result of personality conflicts. If you include such people in leadership positions, you will need to pair them with boundary crossers who can allocate a portion of their energies to detecting and defusing conflicts.

Consider as well the role of charismatic and visionary leaders. Partnerships are frequently initiated and led by what Amey, Eddy, and Ozaki (2007) call "champions" of the partnership, or individuals who can continually promote the effort and inspire participation. These leaders are uniquely charismatic and energetic and play an important role in partnerships because they use their singularity of vision and communication skills to inspire excitement and commitment from the participants. This type of leadership is appropriate for any partnership structure. However, if there is more than one such leader within a partnership, these individuals must be very skillful at working together. They must be able to share the stage and work with the existing visions of their counterparts, integrating both within the overarching vision of the collective. If the leaders are not able or willing to relinquish some of their vision or authority, then consider a limited or coordinative partnership.

## The Professional Allegiances of Leaders

Another factor to consider when selecting leaders is how their professional allegiances may affect the partnership. For instance, each leader will have dual responsibilities and loyalties—primarily to his or her home organization and, secondarily, to the partnership. This tension may be even more acute if the partnership focuses on projects within one of the partnering organizations, in which case that organization's leader probably will feel obligated to think about that school's or IHE's own interests before those of the partnership. At a minimum, consider whether a potential leader is capable of subordinating his or her home organization allegiance to the best interests of the partnership. If not, be aware of this dynamic and ensure that it does not impede the partnership's work. Ideally, choose top leaders who are able to rise above their own allegiances and act on behalf of all constituent identities and who are *perceived* as being able to act in this manner.

In some situations, you may not have the ability to choose top leaders who will be perceived to be able to act in a nonpartisan manner. A common example comes from policy-inspired partnerships. For example, some partnership-based grant programs require that the principal leader of the partnership be a faculty member from one of the STEM disciplines. This means that some of the leaders in these types of partnerships in effect represent a constituency (STEM faculty) that has historically been at odds with some other constituent groups of the partnerships—such as education faculty and K–12 staff. One partnership scholar reported that the primary leader of a project with such a requirement had a very limited understanding of the realities facing K–12 classrooms and also instinctively favored STEM faculty in group discussions. This led some partners to feel marginalized and demoralized (Davis, Feldman, Irwin, Pedevillaro, Weiss, Bray, et al., 2003).

## The Importance of Fostering Distributed Leadership

Partnership work typically cuts across both horizontal and vertical hierarchies, necessitating the involvement of people such as classroom teachers and faculty, college deans, and principals, each of whom must act in some capacity as a leader. Spillane and Diamond (2007) emphasizes this point and argue against the outdated myth of the "hero leader" for any educational organization. They suggest that leadership is best understood as distributed across different people and settings. If the single hero leader is not an apt model within a single organization, it is all the more inappropriate for partnerships and especially collaborative partnerships. Thus, if your partnership has individual leaders who act as the primary source of vision and inspiration, take special steps to emphasize to all your members that these visionary leaders play only one type of leadership role, and that they are not the only important leaders. The partnership we studied provides excellent examples of distributed leadership. UDEP had no fewer than 15 individuals who, during the beginning stages, made key decisions about the partnership. While there was a small group of key top-level leaders, beneath them were people at many levels who actually led the work on the ground. Although this structure might seem cumbersome and overly complex, such an abundance of leaders is useful. It is impossible for a single administrator to understand the details and nuances of all the partnership activities, no matter how indefatigable the person. When leadership is distributed among various people, you benefit from the "two brains are better than one" phenomenon.

## Other Administrative Functions

Two other administrative functions deserve separate and special attention: financial and contractual management, which is a critical governance function, and evaluation, a process that is often poorly understood, designed, and implemented and thus poorly used.

### Financial and Contractual Management

Among the most important administrative decisions required to manage a partnership are those pertaining to the management of finances and contracts. These decisions have to do with who is authorized to oversee the allocation of resources among the various partner organizations. Will budget and contract decisions be made by a single leader or a consensus-based leadership group? If it is a combination of the two, which decisions are to be made by the collective and which by the top leader? Distributing resources among different groups for various tasks is an administratively taxing job and can be an area of conflict or disagreement. Who gets how much money? Who has access to knowledge and staff, and who can tap into relationships and contacts? What are the true costs?

To minimize problems in this area, your partnership should agree on and clearly articulate resource-distribution policies and financial-management procedures. Lack of agreement about performance expectations, fiscal matters, and reporting can be a flash point in a partnership. It is vital to clarify how costs and benefits will be distributed across the partnership. For example, in UDEP, there was a "gentleman's agreement" about distribution of the grant funds. Two leaders agreed ahead of time that portions of the money would be provided to the district partners, and the balance would be split between the two lead IHEs. However, this agreement was not based on a close analysis of the actual work to be undertaken, and thus was not well aligned with the actual work effort. When it became apparent that workload and budget were not well aligned, resentment and distrust emerged. This difficult situation could have been prevented if the parties had agreed at the outset on clear and fair fiscal accountability policies. Partners should also agree on accountability measures and sanctions for nonperformance. These are reasons why it is important to articulate at the outset sound fiscal procedures that all parties agree to and that support your work. Finally, assess the fit between the partnership's proposed activities and processes and the partner organizations' preexisting procedures and policies. For instance, think about the compatibility of bookkeeping procedures, because misaligned accounting or reimbursement processes might have a detrimental effect on the partnership.

---

**Partnership Action Point:** Consider whether partnership financial procedures align with those of the partner organizations.

---

## Evaluation

Both funders and partnership leaders value effective evaluation; yet, many partnership leaders do not understand or value evaluation (Hora, Millar, Arrigoni, & Kretchmar, 2009). To be sure, "measuring" partnerships is difficult. Given the need to develop compelling evidence about partnerships, evaluation plans should provide findings not only on the outcomes of your partnership (i.e., summative evaluation) but also on the processes by which your partnership unfolds (i.e., formative evaluation). We discuss these two types of evaluation next.

*Formative Evaluation*

Formative evaluation focuses on how a program is implemented or delivered. Indicators used in formative evaluation typically include simple counts of program units delivered (e.g., number of workshops held) to ascertain whether the program is proceeding as planned. However, a formative evaluation is not simply about counting heads; it is also a powerful tool that can be used to assess what works and what doesn't as a program is implemented (Patton, 2008). In our experience, partnerships benefit most from a formative evaluation plan that takes a problem-finding stance, because a certain amount of conflict is not only expected but also welcomed in partnerships. You are intentionally bringing together different organizations, with different cultural models, to benefit from the potentially productive effects of managed conflict. Formative evaluation plays a critical role in identifying problems and conflicts as they arise, so immediate action can be taken. As Naida Tushnet (1993) states, an effective evaluation is a problem finder that enables leaders to identify challenges to the work and change course accordingly (p. 83). This can be accomplished if regular reports on the key process indicators (e.g., number of teachers served, number of workshops held) also include information about factors that obstruct or facilitate progress. You need to know as soon as possible whether key objectives are not being met and why, so a group can discuss the issue openly and determine the best course of action. Also, formative evaluation findings can be repurposed as summative assessments and used to report on the effects of specific partnership strategies and to substantiate progress and accomplishments.

However, even the best formative evaluation is of limited value if the partnership's leaders do not have access to the findings or simply ignore them. It is important, therefore, to establish a formal conduit through which your leaders and key personnel obtain formative evaluation data. This can take the form of a recurring item in the central leadership group's regular meeting agenda or direct lines of communication between evaluators and leaders. You must be open to hearing potentially negative findings or data that contradict your own theory of action and to making midcourse corrections. Your evaluator's reports must also be readable and accessible. Some UDEP participants complained that the reports produced by the evaluators were too long and jargon filled to be useful, and others noted that they simply hadn't seen the evaluation reports, which indicated a breakdown in the procedures for disseminating findings. (But some participants, who had easy access to the evaluators, valued and were able to use the formative evaluation findings.)

---

**Partnership Action Point:** Make sure to establish feedback loops where evaluation findings can be delivered quickly to partnership leaders and staff.

---

*Summative Evaluation*

A summative evaluation is used to obtain evidence of a project's ultimate outcomes (e.g., changes in student learning or teacher practices). Evidence of a summative nature is the type most often provided in reports to project funders or stakeholders, to help them assess whether their investments are worthwhile. Thus, it is important to pay careful attention to what types of indicators will be measured as part of your summative evaluation and to ensure that they can in fact be tracked over time to provide compelling evidence of your efforts. One consideration is that although summative evaluation designs typically focus on discrete and easily measured changes, such as student learning or teacher content knowledge (the ultimate goals of many partnership activities), the goal of some partnerships is to develop a collaborative environment that enables *achievement* of these ultimate goals. Achievement of the latter is a far more difficult thing to measure. For instance, your partnership goals might be to create the capacity to achieve change in teacher capacity and student learning. Thus, a summative evaluation designed to measure change in teacher or student outcomes will not line up with your actual partnership goals or provide evidence about the development of internal capacity. UDEP forged new relationships among K–12 schools across the country and between K–12 staff and IHE staff within the same region. These relationships became the foundation for later collaborations that outlasted the grant itself, and that might result in sustainable, deep changes in teacher and student outcomes. However, these relationships were not identified at the outset of the partnership as a desired outcome, so no systematic efforts were taken to evaluate them. Researchers are working to develop indicators to measure changes in organizational learning, such as new knowledge being stored in organizational memory or communicated throughout an organization (Cyert & Goodman, 1997).

Avoid approaching summative evaluation as a perfunctory exercise in satisfying external demands for accountability. Such an approach probably will involve indicators of success that measure only near-term outcomes. Such evaluation also feeds into a quick-fix syndrome that may provide information that ends up hindering achievement of your ultimate goals. As Sirotnik and Goodlad (1988) state, "The enemy of renewal is the quick fix" (p. 224). Instead, focus on more fundamental, albeit longer-term, indicators of success that capture changes in the nature and quality of institutions and individuals.

*Different Tools and Approaches to Partnership Evaluation*

There is growing pressure to improve methodological rigor in program evaluations in education. For instance, some researchers focus on the perceived lack of instruments of demonstrated validity and reliability with which to measure the outcomes of STEM education interventions (Katzenmeyer & Lawrenz, 2006). Given the complex organizational settings in which most partnerships operate, developing compelling evidence for the effects of partnership is a difficult methodological issue. It is challenging to untangle the activities of a partnership from those of home organizations, since many efforts "piggyback" onto existing programs. In response, some researchers and evaluators avoid attributing causality to partnership activities and, instead, use narrative case studies to capture how a partnership operated and to indicate its potential effect on outcomes such as student learning or institutional policy (Waschak & Kingsley, 2006). This approach, which was used in our study of the UDEP partnership, can also be effective in analyzing the processes of partnership operations and their relationship to particular outcomes. However, qualitative analyses of this type can only make claims that are commensurate with the nature of their evidence, so these analyses are not likely to produce strong causal claims.

Other researchers and evaluators use a checklist approach to evaluating partnership activities. For instance, the Center for the Advancement of Collaborative Strategies in Health (2010) developed the "Partnership Self-Assessment Tool," which focuses on capturing a partnership's level of synergy. This tool includes several Likert-style agreement statements (i.e., a five-point scale, from "strongly agree" to "strongly disagree") on topics such as leadership, use of resources, and degree of organizational synergy. Many other evaluation instruments can be found online. We suggest you scan the available tools to get ideas and then adapt or borrow from an existing evaluation framework or instrument. Below are some key points to consider when designing your evaluation.

> **Partnership Action Point:** Ensure adequate funding for your program evaluation; carefully identify formative and outcome indicators; and take into account more affective measures, such as changes in trust among groups.

First, decide how much money to spend on evaluation. There is no rule of thumb regarding the amount of funding to set aside for evaluation, because each partnership will have a different resource base and situation (O'Sullivan, 2004). That said, be mindful that if you shortchange your evaluation activities, you probably will disappoint your funders or stakeholders and hamper your overall effectiveness.

Second, decide as precisely as possible what to measure as evidence of a partnership's efficacy. Begin by deciding on the organizational level on which you will focus: the entire partnership, one partner organization, a working group, or an individual. An evaluation at the group level might provide evidence of the way outcomes at the leadership level trickle down throughout the entire partnership. By contrast, an evaluation conducted at the partnership level as a whole is less likely to expose the differences within working groups. Unless you address these issues at the outset, you will be in the uncomfortable position of determining what to measure and how to justify your efforts to a funder or policy maker in the middle of the project period (Hora et al., 2009). You should revisit your evaluation design regularly to ensure that it continues to meet your partnership's needs and is implemented adequately.

Third, consider including both traditional outcome measures (e.g., changes in teacher knowledge) and organizational process and affective measures that can capture the more qualitative effects of partnership work. These might include indicators such as changes in the level of trust among groups and in the size of social or professional networks. An evaluation design that includes both types of indicators will be able to assess a partnership's success at achieving its longer-term goals and generative partnership processes, including the behavioral and subjective aspects of partnership. The aforementioned Partnership Self-Assessment Tool is a good example of an approach that captures affective outcomes, in this case the degree of organizational synergy.

Finally, some organizational researchers are shifting from an exclusive focus on individual-level change, known as the "effectiveness model" of evaluation, toward accounting for changes in organizational procedures and structures, which exert significant influence on educational behaviors over time (e.g., Patton, 2006). Studying individual-level change is good, but not sufficient, since a project can stimulate many changes at the organizational level that may support (or inhibit) individual learning. A narrow focus on student or teacher change may miss these outcomes (Mintzberg, Dougherty, Jorgensen, & Westley, 1996). Thus, partnerships that tackle systemic change, such as changing entire school districts' instructional practices, need evaluations that gather information about the types of changes that may lead to change in the system as a whole. That is, instead of focusing on outcomes such as student learning, identify processes that improve instruction at the classroom level, such as teacher professional development or district support systems.

## Chapter Summary

> **Core Idea:** Partnerships are not self-administering enterprises. You cannot safely assume that the procedures and leadership styles that work in your home organization will transfer to the 3rd space of partnership. Instead, you must choose decision-making procedures, leaders, and other administrative functions that enable achievement of the new partnership's goals and objectives while also being compatible with partner organization norms.

### *Governance*

- Governance consists of the processes, customs, and policies by which an organization is administered and makes decisions.
- The main models for governance in partnerships are top-down and consensus-based. Each of these is best suited to particular organizational structures, and most partnerships use a hybrid of these two models.
- Top-down governance is common in schools and can be effective in partnerships. If this model is used, you should have a single decision maker.

- Shared and consensus-based governance is common in universities and requires a participatory decision-making process and high levels of trust. This type of governance is not easy, particularly in the 3rd space of partnership work.
- Clear lines of authority, permissible types of actions, and sanctions for noncompliance must be established.

## Selecting Leaders

- Consider leadership styles, professional allegiances, and boundary-crossing abilities when you select leaders for partnership work.
- Match leadership styles with partnership structure (e.g., a limited partnership is well suited to a leader with a top-down style).
- Determine whether leaders are capable of subordinating their allegiance to their home organization to their allegiance to the partnership.
- Choose leaders who recognize that leadership in a partnership should be distributed across many organizations and working groups.

## Other Administrative Functions

- Clarify how and by whom financial and contractual management issues will be handled.
- Carefully craft an evaluation plan at the beginning of the partnership, designing it to provide both formative findings, which identify problems and gauge the progress of the work, and summative findings, which capture the entirety of the partnership's accomplishments.
- Include organizational process and affective (e.g., increased trust in the collective) measures as well as outcome (e.g., number of new working groups) measures.

## Bibliographic Note

There is substantial literature on governance and administration in organization science, administrative science, and several other fields. For discussions on governance and administrative issues specific to collaborative work, see Gray (1989) and Thomson and Perry (2006). For a discussion of the key nature of determining boundaries in interorganizational relations, see Ring and Van de Ven (1994). For references to shared governance as an important facet of partnership work, see Sirotnik and Goodlad (1988). For a discussion about effective information sharing and its importance to group operations (a subject developed in greater detail in chapter 7), see Perkins (1993). For a discussion about visionary leaders in partnerships and their relative strengths and weaknesses, see Amey et al. (2007). For a case study about an education partnership in which tensions between STEM faculty and others became evident, see Davis, Feldman, Irwin, Pedevillano, Weiss, Bray, et al. (2003).

We cite here just a few of the many resources available for program evaluators. Patton's 2008 book, *Utilization-Focused Evaluation*, provides a solid overview of the field and the different types of evaluation approaches that can be used to increase the utility and impact of program evaluations. Of particular relevance to partnership work is O'Sullivan (2004), which also provides an overview of program evaluation and how it can be used in collaborative situations. See Miles and Huberman (1994) for a discussion on causation in qualitative research. See Huber (1991) for a discussion of the key components of organizational learning, and Cyert and Goodman (1997) for an analysis of how to evaluate changes effectively in organizational learning. For discussions of the need to adopt a systemic approach in evaluating educational reforms, see Anderson and Helms (2001), Patton (2006), and Resnick et al. (2007).

# 7

# EFFECTIVE COMMUNICATION SYSTEMS

Hierarchies can be smart, and democracies can
be dumb. It's not just the structures that matter,
but the people and operating styles within them.

(Perkins, 2003, p. 12)

C ommunication systems underlie almost every aspect of partnership
operations and functions. They can provide a way to disseminate
information throughout the partnership, work through conflicts,
and create relationships among individuals across the partnership. However,
when communication systems are ineffective, partnerships and other types
of collaborative work are unlikely to be successful.

A group's communication system won't necessarily be effective just
because the group uses the most up-to-date information and communication
technology (e.g., wireless hardware, online wikis, voice-activated software)
or the most rational and organized routines and procedures (e.g., regular
weekly meetings, monthly reporting requirements), because the elements of
the communication system do not guarantee the value of the information
being conveyed. As management scientist Henry Mintzberg and his colleagues (1996) say, real collaboration is "psychic" and is grounded in the
"mysterious chemistry of human interaction" (p. 62). This interaction is
both enabled and shaped by a group's cultural models. On the other hand,
you can hamper your partnership needlessly by not investing in available
information and communication technologies that can improve your communication processes. The hardware, software, and procedures you select
for your partnership communications system will affect how efficiently and
effectively people share information and interact.

The key to creating an effective communication system is to identify the
kind of communication outcomes needed to achieve your partnership goals,

and then develop the right combination of (1) infrastructure elements (i.e., structures and technologies, routines and procedures), and (2) cultural models. Remember to identify preexisting infrastructural elements and cultural models that are part of "the way things are done" in each partner organization. Then identify the organizational and cultural boundaries you need to span and respect. You might need to invest substantial resources to identify the processes and mechanisms that fit the specific needs of your partnership, and then adapt these processes into routines that serve you well.

---

**Partnership Action Point:** Identify the norms, procedures, and technologies that are part of "the way things are done" in each partner organization and then locate the organizational and cultural boundaries you need to span and respect.

---

An organization's communication infrastructure creates the occasions and roles through which people connect, or as David Perkins (2003) puts it, the "contact architecture" (p. 36). Examples include peers meeting face-to-face in the mail room, a group of department chairs meeting with the provost or principal in a formal meeting room, a workplace veteran giving impromptu advice to a newcomer over coffee, or the human resources director sending an e-mail to the full staff about a new procedure. These opportunities for interaction are enabled by an organization's communications infrastructure, which includes the organization's physical space. As individuals interact with one another over time and develop routines related to particular tasks (e.g., lesson planning, curriculum development), new cultural models are created that eventually become taken-for-granted ways of doing things (Halverson, 2003). Thus, we encourage you to view the creation of a partnership communications system not only as a necessary administrative chore but also as an opportunity for creating more meaningful interactions among the people in your group and for fostering new cultural dynamics.

## Working With Existing Systems

The first step in building your partnership communications system is to work with the partners' existing systems. This requires taking stock of their communication infrastructures, including the hierarchies and networks through which communication flows, the communication routines used by relevant affinity groups, and the cultural models operating in each group. Based on these preexisting conditions, you can tailor your partnership procedures accordingly.

### Identify Your Partners' Communication Systems

A good place to start when identifying the elements of partners' communication systems is to catalogue the key components of each partner organization's system, which include, but are not limited to, the following:

- Types of information technology (hardware and software) and use patterns: For example, if you discover that a K–12 district primarily uses a PC-based system, and that all classroom teachers have Dell laptops hooked up to a school-based server, you probably should not design a Mac-based system for the partnership. You must also find out whether the teachers use their computers as their main mode of communication with one another and administrators or if other means of communication are more important (e.g., person-to-person communication at weekly staff meetings).
- Meetings and other types of interaction structures: Find out how relevant organizational units (e.g., science department, school board, and curriculum and instruction department) meet and conduct business. Do they meet regularly in person, with frequent e-mails and texting between meetings? Or do they meet only by conference call when a crisis emerges? Do the group members tend to gather over a beer every Friday afternoon? Be aware that these patterns form a backdrop for people from these groups as they interact in your 3rd space of partnership.

Additionally, you should identify the prevailing cultural models for communication. David Perkins (2003) has introduced a simple and useful way to think about the cultural models that shape human interactions within communication systems. He writes that there are "progressive interactions" and "regressive interactions." The former enable you to make progress toward your goals, and the latter slow things down or send things backward (p. 20). Unfortunately, Perkins's research—which is confirmed by our experience—supports the conclusion that in community and organizational contexts, regressive interactions tend to predominate. Whether progressive or regressive, these interaction processes tend to be particularly resilient as a result of being internalized into mental models and cultural models, and

then reinforced through organizational routines and made visible into artifacts such as policies and procedures.

> **Partnership Action Point:** Determine whether your partners' com-
> munication systems are effective, and if not, cautiously introduce
> alternative technologies and nurture more progressive cultural mod-
> els for communication.

It is also useful to try to determine whether partners consider their communication system to be effective and whether you agree with their assessments. If the quality of communication is poor, you might want to
cautiously introduce alternative technologies and nurture more progressive
cultural models for communication. In the event that existing communications are regressive, then you also will want to avoid integrating these practices into the 3rd space of partnership. For instance, if a university
department is known for a lack of timely and accurate information dissemi-
nation to faculty and staff, then you should not adopt its procedures. If
under-the-table back talk is the cultural model that prevails in the top eche-
lon of a school's administration, you must make clear that, in your partnership, people put their issues on the table and interact respectfully as they
address these issues.

### Note How Communication Systems Vary in Hierarchical and Flat Organizations

Working with educational organizations means that you inevitably will have
to deal with the unique organizational systems of K–12 schools and districts
and IHEs. Consider the case of strongly hierarchical organizations that have
clear reporting lines or are highly segmented. In such organizations, the
contact architecture tends to be relatively coherent, expressing the hierarchical organizational structure. Roles, protocols, and spaces are well defined,
and it is relatively easy to figure out who talks to whom, about what, and
using which interaction and meeting protocols and which spaces and circumstances. For example, a first-year teacher in such an organization knows
that it would take an emergency for him or her to interrupt the superintendent's meeting with the board of directors. However, such clarity often
comes with a rigidity that prevents top decision makers from rapidly gathering the information and diversity of perspectives they need to make good
decisions in a fast-paced, competitive environment.

By contrast, consider the contact architecture of organizations with more horizontal governance structures and more permeable boundaries between units and roles. Although far more ambiguous and challenging to navigate, this kind of contact architecture allows leaders at all levels to mobilize knowledge, resources, and other people rapidly and creatively to gather information and make inspired and good decisions. On the other hand, the lack of clarity and the random nature of this kind of system can also make it difficult to get even routine things accomplished (Birnbaum, 1991). The protocols, roles, and spaces are not aligned well enough to consistently promote interactions among people who have valuable information and ideas to share. Individuals may be inundated with certain types of information they do not need and be left entirely out of information loops in which they should participate. The left hand may not know what the right hand is doing, and the organization operates with inefficient parallel processes.

Besides examining the hierarchies within organizations, it is also important to study the relative positions of the different organizations within your partnership. This is particularly important for organizations that have developed relationships with one another already. In each case, determine the lines of communication and ascertain whether these relationships are hierarchical or flat, and whether these preexisting relationships will influence the partnership as it unfolds. Also consider that partner organizations with embedded relationships may want to maintain exclusive oversight or control of their preexisting arrangements. For instance, communicating with partner contacts became an issue for the senior leadership group of UDEP when one leader became engaged in a conversation with a district administrator at a meeting and offered technical assistance in response to this administrator's request for help. Another UDEP leader, who had a preexisting relationship with the district, viewed this contact as a violation of his organization's autonomy. His group had made clear that it would act as the "gatekeeper" in all interactions with members of this district. In response to this incident, the organization drafted a set of communication protocols that laid out even more clearly who was allowed to speak to district staff.

## Creating a Progressive Partnership Communication System

Communication systems not only enable sharing of information but also enable and shape personal interactions. Research on characteristics of partnership success in the business sector often highlights the importance of high-quality communication, in which important information is shared quickly and efficiently. Regardless of the partnership type you have chosen, the communication system can make or break your partnership, and establishing a good system will be challenging. That said, the 3rd space may also offer new opportunities to step away from some of the less effective systems and practices that prevail in your home organization and to start fresh with new colleagues. A partnership will develop its own contact architecture and interaction processes, which provides a golden opportunity to support progressive modes of communicating and interacting and to neutralize regressive ones.

## Beware of the Downsides of Digital Communication Technology

As you well know, 21st-century organizations are increasingly shaped by the digital information technologies they use. These technologies include online work spaces that house complex databases, audiovisual resources, video communication systems ranging from Skype to 3-D caves, and constant-contact technologies like Twitter. Like most technologies, these can have a net positive impact on the 3rd space of partnership, fostering progressive interactions in powerful and effective ways. Sometimes, however, they can inhibit meaningful interactions among individuals and groups within a partnership.

Because these technologies' strengths tend to be well known, we call attention here to their potential weakness. First, e-mail should not be viewed as the principal means of communication in a partnership. It should not be used at all for topics that are extremely important or potentially contentious and where personal interactions are essential to avoid misunderstandings. In the UDEP project, reliance on e-mail became a serious problem, because it exacerbated existing tensions and contributed to information overload for many participants. Overreliance on e-mail can short-circuit nonverbal communication and face-to-face time, which are essential components of building relationships, camaraderie, and trust. Organizational researcher Henry Mintzberg and colleagues (1996) note the difference between a senior manager who spends two hours a day at home communicating with staff via e-mail and a manager who continually engages his or her staff in conversations and on-the-spot problem solving. The latter type of manager is able to deal with problems in the moment instead of having to wait to deal with them at scheduled meetings, by which time they are probably days old and will have to be sandwiched between a variety of other pressing topics.

Partnership Action Point: Use e-mail to complement regular face-to-face interactions, not as the principal mode of interaction.

Second, audio-only and "screen" technologies used for synchronous long-distance meetings are prone to breaking down. During the early stages of the UDEP partnership, several important meetings were held by video-conferencing, so that individuals from K–12 districts and universities from across the country could participate. Unfortunately, the system faltered, and some people were unable to be seen or heard, which shut them out of the meetings. Because audio-only and screen meetings not only omit the important personal touch but also run the risk of technical breakdown, they should be used to augment, not replace, the crucial face-to-face meetings that are a building block of partnership.

## *Design for Effective Meetings*

Running effective meetings is an abiding principle of organizational management in every field. In a 2009 interview Shantanu Narayan, CEO and president of Adobe Systems, said that meetings are not for sharing reams of data and then having leaders make pronouncements but for discussing what people want to accomplish, what is and isn't working in the business, and what people's concerns are. Furthermore, he argues that a leader's role is to create a venue for participants to safely voice their opinions and needs, a process that can build ownership and encourage involvement in the work. Thus, at the outset, establish effective meeting procedures. This entails deciding where meetings will take place, who should attend, and how these meetings will be facilitated.

We recommend that you identify what you want to accomplish at a meeting and then structure the agenda to achieve these outcomes. This will help you keep the meeting focused, foster productive dialogue, and avoid a litany of individuals simply reporting on their recent activities, which can make meetings boring and ineffective. Make the dialogue visible—have someone at a whiteboard writing down important ideas and points as they come up. Once ideas are physically in front of the group, they will no longer seem as tied to the individuals who brought them up, and the group will be more likely to accept them. Finally, try to have fun in meetings. The members of the UDEP science professional-development group started each meeting by talking about one thing each of them had done for fun since the last meeting. This was a natural way to establish a personal rapport.

A group might want to hold meetings regularly if continuing conversation, such as when the group is in the midst of a flurry of collaborative work, is important. At one point the science professional-development group, whose members were located in different cities, held weekly conference calls. This not only enabled all group members to touch base but also enabled members to share ideas, troubleshoot, and develop personal friendships. Some meetings were structured so that all participants came as learners, and the leaders made certain that participants did not try to outshine one another. Participants described other meetings as "open learning environments" (more about ideas than content), ones in which participants were encouraged to see all ideas as valid. However effective communication procedures, such as regular meetings or e-mail protocols may be lacking or are untenable because of organizational or cultural differences. It might not be feasible for a principal or lead teacher to attend regular meetings or respond to every e-mail pertaining to the project. Moreover, additional planning or troubleshooting sessions may be needed even when regular meetings among partners provide a venue for cross-organizational dialogue. Research has found that in these cases, boundary-crossing leaders who are actively engaged in the work can fill the gap and act as communication links (Burt, 1992). However, if a partnership lacks such leaders, the absence of formal structures will inhibit effective communication among partner groups.

> **Partnership Action Point:** Develop an agenda with specific outcomes to structure your meetings, have someone write all ideas on a board to depersonalize topics, and emphasize fun!

## *Select for and Foster Effective Communication Styles*

We all can provide examples of positive and negative communication styles exhibited by education leaders; we offer just a few here. People with positive communication styles evidence respect for others in tone and demeanor and take the time to provide the right amount of information to the right people in a timely manner. They listen and observe carefully so they can identify other people's mental models. They avoid making unwarranted assumptions and use techniques such as rephrasing to confirm that they understand what others intend. They are responsive, honest, and compassionate and have a sense of humor, and they are committed to achieving the organization's goals in ways that minimize harm to specific individuals. These attributes resemble those of effective boundary crossers, as described in chapter 4. You know when you are in the presence of people who use positive communication styles because you and others enjoy interacting with them. Colleagues are inclined to trust them and to feel safe enough in their presence to take risks by offering creative ideas. They inspire loyalty, and their colleagues are inclined to go out of their way to provide useful information and to work harder, longer, and smarter to achieve goals.

By contrast, people whose communication styles are confrontational, disparaging of others, disrespectful in tone, or arrogant tend to reduce the effectiveness of work in the 3rd space. These individuals may lack compassion and may place their own self-interest above the interests of the organization. Colleagues tend to respond to them with fear, avoidance, resentment, and cynicism. Instead of loyalty, they elicit wordless compliance, loss of confidence and interest, or passive resistance. Good ways to help limit the negative effect of such individuals are to point out their behavior to them as soon as possible, preferably in private, but if necessary in public, and to explain directly to them how their style affects individuals and groups.

In sum, try to select participants with positive communication styles, establish cultural models and routines within your partnership that encourage positive communication interactions, and find ways to minimize the effects of people with negative communication styles.

### Create a Common Language Among Different Affinity Groups

Effectively crafted partnership communication systems will shape how people interact and work on partnership tasks. Over time, these regular interactions may lead to the development of a common vision and new cultural models for the work. Although creating a new affinity group is difficult and might not be desirable or necessary for your partnership, at the very least you should strive to create a common language among working group participants. One participant in the UDEP partnership noted that in prior partnerships, shared work across many districts had led to a common language, so in these earlier partnerships he could communicate easily with colleagues about curriculum and professional development across all school sites. Groups with different languages and jargon will present a major communication problem, and developing a shared vocabulary to discuss the work will be challenging. The process of forging this common vocabulary also lays the foundation for establishing a group identity, a key aspect of group development and trust.

## Chapter Summary

**Core Idea:** Communication systems underlie almost every aspect of partnership operations and functions. Creating an effective system requires building on the norms, procedures, and technologies that are part of the way things are done in each partner organization. Identifying the communication infrastructure (e.g., technology and procedures) and behavioral norms (e.g., cultural models for interaction) that best fit these preexisting systems will foster meaningful and productive interactions within your partnership.

### *Working With Existing Communication Systems*

- For all participating organizations, identify existing communication infrastructures, including information technology systems and how individuals interact and meet.
- In hierarchical organizations, pay close attention to authority lines and how different administrative units and levels communicate with one another.
- Take careful note of the relationships in which your partners are embedded and consider whether and how these relationships will affect the partnership (e.g., some contacts may be off limits to the collective).

### *Creating a Progressive Partnership Communication System*

- Carefully integrate information technologies (e.g., e-mail, videoconferencing) into your partnership and encourage people to communicate face-to-face whenever possible.
- Hold effective meetings by making sure your agendas reflect shared notions of the rationale for a given meeting and that the meetings use people's limited time and resources effectively.
- Create a common vocabulary within the partnership, because miscommunication arising from inability to understand organizational

or disciplinary jargon is common and can inhibit the formation of a collective identity and trust.

## Bibliographic Note

Organization and administrative sciences scholars have long studied communication and its role in collaborative work. For a robust overview of communication as the underpinning to partnerships and other interorganizational arrangements, see Gray (1989). For discussions of the role of effective communications in collaborative work, see Barringer and Harrison (2000); Mattessich, Murray-Close, and Monsey (2001); Mintzberg et al. (1996); and Mohr and Spekman (1994). In this chapter we draw heavily on the work of David Perkins (2003); his analysis of developing progressive interactions seems particularly salient to partnership work. Thomson and Perry (2006) provide a good overview of the need to tailor communication systems to local needs and conditions. See Ostrom (1998) for a focus on the importance of personal contacts and face-to-face time in collaborative work. The interview with Shantanu Narayan appeared in the Corner Office column in the Sunday Business section of the *New York Times* on July 19, 2009. Finally, for a good resource regarding how leaders should approach communications, see Hamm (2006).

# PART THREE

---

# IMPLEMENTING PARTNERSHIPS

I used to think that running an organization was
equivalent to conducting a symphony orchestra.
But I don't think that's quite it; it's more like jazz.
There is more improvisation.

(Warren Bennis, *Flight Plan for Leaders*, 1994).

Now that you have designed your partnership, you can shift your focus to implementing the strategies you believe will accomplish your goals. We would like to be able to assure you that if you have worked through all the preliminary steps presented in the foregoing six chapters all that remains is to oversee these organizational structures and processes. To make such a claim, however, would be misleading. At most, we can assure you that this up-front work provides needed structure, reduces the unpredictability endemic to the 3rd space of partnership, and prepares you to manage the inevitable tension and change that are hallmarks of partnership work. The policies and organizational structures you and other partnership leaders put into place at the very beginning will need to be renegotiated repeatedly as partners get to know one another, as individuals join and leave, as the nature of the tasks evolves, and as trust and a collective identity are created (or not). As you establish work protocols, settle conflicts, handle funds, and make adjustments in response to unexpected external disruptions, such as an economic crisis, your partnership will change continually.

The emergent and unpredictable nature of partnership work contributes to partnerships presenting unique challenges that test even the most experienced leaders. As one participant told us, "I don't like partnerships—they're too difficult to pull off." Another told us simply, "I try to avoid them at all costs." The kaleidoscope of cultural models, structures and technologies, routines and practices, resources, and personalities that partner organizations bring into the 3rd space creates a milieu in which anything can happen (Morgan, 1998). And, of course, partnership activities must be squeezed into participants' already demanding schedules, which are filled with routine curricular, personnel, and budget decisions and administrative fires that need to be extinguished. This is why one of the participants in the UDEP partnership described the work as akin to "jumping on a moving train."

With these conditions in mind, we draw on our own research and the research literature to seek guidelines for implementing partnerships. Because of the unpredictability of partnership work, individuals who possess adaptive expertise will be able to more effectively craft solutions to the inevitable cascade of challenges and opportunities than will individuals with limited capacity to change. Thus, expect to work hard and outside your comfort zone. In this part of the book, we hope to help you learn to design partnership work, create and manage groups, and address the critical issues of trust and conflict.

# 8

# DESIGNING THE WORK

While preparing for and designing your partnership, you probably discussed how to design and undertake the work needed to actually implement your strategies. How will you develop these new course materials? What math lessons are out there, and which ones are suitable for our professional-development workshops? What textbook should we use in redesigning the course on arithmetical problem solving? You and your partners have probably hashed out some details like this already; it gives people a sense of accomplishment to focus on these practical and tangible things. Although this chapter comes late in the book, the actual work of the partnership should be discussed early in the partnership-planning process. Engaging in real work will draw out different groups' cultural models, which should influence your selection of an organizational structure and other administrative procedures. The sooner the work begins, the sooner the group can move from faux collaboration to actual collaborative interactions.

It is not our goal to provide guidance about the specific strategies, tasks, or activities your partnership should adopt or engage in. You can get such information from journals, books, and experts in the relevant field. Instead, we emphasize a particular strategy for approaching task design, which is to tailor the work to local conditions and to focus your energies on changing strategically selected leverage points in the organization or system. This approach is based on the fact that designing partnership work is rarely just a matter of deciding on a particular task and executing it. If the focus and design of your work is insensitive to local conditions, you may get a weak response from the faculty or teachers you hope will engage with and benefit from your work. Change is hard. A necessary, although not sufficient, condition is understanding whether the school or IHE where you hope people will actually participate in your program or use the resource you develop are generally *ready* for change, and specifically ready for the change your partnership has in mind (Fullan, 2001). Is the district, given its unique politics and funding issues, the right place for this particular initiative? Is there something about this university that requires a shift in how you're framing the problem? Because each of your partnership working groups will operate in a new shared territory that will be "foreign" to some group members, you need to begin by engaging in a little ethnographic legwork. To maximize the prospects that your efforts will find a receptive audience, you must ensure that the work is linked to the realities of daily practice in classrooms and lecture halls.

Thus, it is crucial to identify the key characteristics (including technologies and cultural models) of the school or IHE where the activity will unfold because it is there that the determination will be made about how the intervention is received and ultimately adopted (or not). Once the partnership ends, the people in these organizations must implement and sustain the project or intervention. If the individuals in the task environment don't see a need for what the partnership can offer, or if they think the time is wrong, they will not buy into the project. In this chapter, we offer four guidelines to help you design the partnership tasks in a way that maximizes the alignment of the work to local conditions: (1) understand the task environment, (2) select a leverage point, (3) identify the right type of intervention, and (4) build bridges to all levels of the local partner organization. A core idea is to become an organizational ethnographer and to listen, gather data, and learn about the stakeholders in the place where the work will unfold.

> **Partnership Action Point:** Understand the task environment, select a leverage point, identify the right type of intervention, and build bridges to all levels of the local partner organization.

## Understand the Task Environment

One participant who had never had a good experience in partnership summed up partnerships in this way: "Here, let me use up a lot of your time and effort on something that we already know isn't going to work."

(Middle-school teacher)

A core element of our approach to partnership planning is to develop a deep understanding of each partner's unique organizational and cultural characteristics. It is now time to focus on the "task environment," by which we mean the specific venues that are the focus of your partnership, whether mathematics classrooms, professional-development workshops, or an entire system of teacher training within a district. Although members of the partner organizations who already operate within these task environments will take for granted the cultural models, structures, and routines that prevail there, many members of your partnership probably will not have a working knowledge of these places, and people in the task environments might have little working knowledge of activities that are taking place across the hall from them.

The benefits of understanding local conditions and stakeholders are many. Such understanding conveys to your partners that you place a high value on getting to know local issues and local personalities, and that you can demonstrate it through your physical presence at local meetings or events, or through a solid grasp of local issues that comes through in your conversations. This message can be particularly important for K–12 staff to hear; they may be accustomed to being ignored or overlooked when it comes to the actual design and implementation of reform projects that directly affect them. For instance, when a leader from the science professional-development group of UDEP asked an administrator in the district for a copy of the proposal for a recent grant for science education, the man was flabbergasted and said, "This is the first time someone from a university showed that they believed we district folks could do good work on our own!" It seems that many K–12 educators are accustomed to their higher education counterparts simply developing curricula or workshops, which are then "thrown over the wall," with little cooperative planning to ensure that these creations actually meet local needs. According to one UDEP participant, "It's very powerful when leaders spend time getting to know what is really going on locally, instead of looking at things solely from a numbers or statistics standpoint." This individual commented that a UDEP administrator from an IHE regularly visited the individual's district and came to know the key personalities, local politics, and pressing issues.

**Partnership Action Point:** A core principle of successful partnership work is to ensure that activities fit the local context and meet the needs of local educators.

## Rely on Others to Help You Understand the Task Environment

Be sure to involve other people in your efforts to understand the task environment, because understanding the nuances and complexities of a new place or group of people isn't something one person can do effectively. Consider adopting the anthropological method of identifying and then approaching a "key informant," that is, a staff person or administrator with deep local knowledge who can take you around and show you the lay of the land. Ask your local experts to be as specific as they can about the origins of the problem, how parties are involved or affected, the geographic areas involved, and how different groups influence both the problem and any potential solution. Make sure that all working group members receive this information from the local experts. You might want to ask your program evaluator to provide findings from baseline and progress data-collection efforts as soon as possible, so you can use these findings to assess how well aligned your project is with the task environment. As Naida Tushnet (1993) states, "Successful educational partnerships use evaluation and strategic and adaptive planning to ensure that activities meet local needs and conditions" (p. 27). Understanding the task environment is not a onetime process, like a needs assessment that is conducted at the beginning of a project and then shelved, never to be consulted again. Instead, this is an ongoing process of becoming more informed.

## Widen Your Scope to Include the Broader Context of Education

Understanding the local task environment also entails understanding the larger contexts that affect and shape this environment. Things like budgetary crises or a spike in gang-related violence in a particular city will affect the teachers, faculty, staff, and administrators who participate in your partnership. The national context of higher and K–12 education and federal education policy, teacher unions, school boards, and disciplinary societies (e.g., math, biology education) may also influence your partnership and its participants. While some of these contextual factors might exert only a subtle influence on your participants, others might directly affect its identity and operations. In any case, it is important to be aware that these contexts constitute the political, economic, and sociocultural landscape in which local participants operate. If you don't understand these contexts, you probably will miss key facets of the organizational reality in which you are working and will be puzzled why people make certain decisions.

## *Focus on the History of Educational Reform*

Understanding the legacy of past reforms is important because they influence participants' perspectives (Tushnet, 1993). If past efforts failed and left negative expectations and cynicism, you can try to avoid repeating these mistakes and demonstrate clearly how your efforts will be different. If prior efforts were successful, you can build on them and perhaps save or redirect time and resources. If people associated with earlier efforts are still in the system, attempt to engage them as allies. Otherwise, they are likely to view you as naïve competitors. Don't rely solely on summative project reports of past efforts; often, information about successful processes is omitted because the processes are not easily measured, and information about failures is omitted because failures reflect badly on the project. Another factor to consider is whether other projects are simultaneously operating in the task environment. In particular, you need to find out whether other groups are engaging in projects involving the same teachers or faculty as those who are involved in your partnership to avoid unnecessary "respondent burden." As UDEP began, two related grant-based projects were under way in one of the districts, and it was important for UDEP staff to understand what these projects were doing, so they did not duplicate efforts.

## *Craft Authentic Tasks for Your Partnership*

Use this information to inform partnership leaders and to craft activities and tasks that will reach your target population. A significant amount of research on learning shows that activities and problems that resemble the real-world experiences of students lead to stronger learning and retention (National Research Council, 2000). This is particularly true for adults, who tend not to use new knowledge and methods unless they learn them while engaging in meaningful tasks that directly apply to their workplaces. Thus, partnerships seeking to change classroom teaching or organizational procedures should use "authentic tasks," that is, interventions that relate to the daily needs and challenges that local educators face and that provide solutions to commonly perceived problems.

## Select a Leverage Point

Our second guideline for designing the work pertains to identifying the groups and individuals in the task environment who will give your work the greatest leverage. These leverage points may be individuals such as the superintendent, the people who set departmental policy, or individual teachers who are opinion leaders. They may also be structural points, such as an interdepartmental committee overseeing teacher-training policies or the population of underrepresented students from community colleges who might transfer to four-year IHEs. Where in the hierarchy are the decisions that most pertain to your goals made, and who are the influential individuals? Ask your local experts to help you decide whether it's best to work with people at the top, the middle, or the bottom rungs of organizations. Identify which departments or individuals are the true decision makers or represent leverage points that will bring the most "bang for the buck." The point is to be strategic, clear, and informed and to use evidence (or a strong theory of action) to identify leverage points that will enable you to use your scarce resources to best effect. Also, remain open to the possibility that the results from your analysis of the task environment may require you to revise your theory of action.

The first thing to decide is where in the organizational hierarchy you should focus your task group's work: the top, middle, or bottom. If the task environment you choose involves an entire organization, the upper-level administration probably will be the optimal leverage point. For instance, one of the partner universities in UDEP had a theory of action focused on developing a coherent mathematics curriculum that could be adopted by an entire urban district. The partner believed that, because of the high level of student mobility in urban districts, this type of centralized curriculum was necessary to ensure that all district students received the same quality and type of instruction. The partner also believed that a district-wide professional-development program was needed to support the teachers in using this centralized curriculum. Given this district-wide task environment, the partner selected top-level administrators as its leverage point and focused on shifting the thinking and policies of these individuals. For districts or universities with strong (and experienced) administrators, this may make sense. However, in situations in which upper-level management is less influential or less stable, another strategy may be more effective. For instance, in departments with strong traditions of autonomy within the college or university, a president-centered strategy probably will be less effective.

Another UDEP working group chose to operate at the middle level of the organization. Cindy, the leader of the science professional-development group, chose to focus on middle-level management after spending hundreds of hours figuring out the lay of the land and talking with key informants in the district. She and her working group colleagues came to understand that decisions about the science program were made within two preexisting organizational units: the elementary science group and the secondary science group. Both groups included experienced teachers charged with providing professional development for teacher colleagues. These were the people best equipped to develop better classroom-level science resources, and who best understood the cultural and structural constraints of the schools and district. With agreement from top administrators, Cindy and her colleagues decided to collaborate closely with these midlevel educators rather than work directly with top-level administrators who were far removed from classroom teachers.

Another leverage point is the grassroots level, which in education entities often is the classroom personnel—classroom teachers in K–12 schools and faculty or instructional staff in IHEs. Partnerships or task groups that hold a bottom-up theory of change and believe that improvement starts with, and depends on, the people and processes at the classroom level are likely to look for leverage points at this level. For example, a partnership whose goal is to develop local professional learning communities that are capable of providing the resources and support instructors need to improve their teaching practice should pick a grassroots-level leverage point. Other task groups may work at this level because they do not have the desire, resources, or permission to attempt change that directly affects broader organizational units. In any case, if you work at this level, you may identify local teacher opinion leaders or individual teachers and specific classroom procedures as your leverage point.

## Identify the Right Type of Intervention

Determine the type of intervention your partnership should undertake by considering the nature of the problem and your partnership's goals and objectives. Many factors must be considered when choosing the right type of intervention. Here we bring special attention to just one factor: the nature of the problem.

Technical problems usually are clearly understood, and the processes and technologies for addressing them are well established and have been proved effective based on research or other evidence. For instance, research indicates that the traditional single-day workshop with no follow-up is not effective, whereas professional-development for K–12 teachers that is both in-depth and on-going is effective. In particular, the research on professional development schools indicates that preservice teachers benefit from increases in the length of their field experience and the amount and quality of supervision and feedback. In situations where you have this kind of clear identification of a problem, and established processes for addressing it, you have a technical problem. That being said, it may not be so simple to solve the problem. For example, in specific local conditions, a multiday series of workshops may not be feasible because of budgetary limitations or a constrained academic calendar. Indeed, one-size-fits-all solutions rarely work well in education, and even a well-established model, such as professional-development schools, will need to be adapted to fit local needs, conditions, and constraints.

Indeed, many education partnerships address adaptive, rather than technical, problems. An adaptive challenge is one that even the best experts have not defined clearly, let alone solved. Resolving such challenges requires the collaboration of a diverse range of experts and participants, which is why these types of problems warrant the effort involved in forming partnerships. When working on an adaptive challenge, you should choose an intervention *strategy*, not an intervention. You need to take a more iterative and creative approach to problem solving, and your approach should engage local experts and users every step of the way. A downside of this approach is that it entails expensive development and testing, and the end result may still not be a mature technology that can be adapted easily elsewhere. Thus, although the intervention you develop may garner local ownership, it also is likely to be risky and expensive. The upside, however, is that your partnership will not end up forcing an inappropriate mature technology in an environment that will actively resist it.

## Build Bridges to All Levels of the Local Partner Organization

Our last guideline for designing the work is to build bridges to people at all levels of the local organization. Taking the time to build bridges will provide multiple benefits. It is easy not to engage in this communication task, but you cannot afford to overlook this work. Two facets of bridge-building work are especially important: communicating with all levels to establish lines of communication while also conveying interest, and paying attention to how information is framed and conveyed to specific audiences.

## Establishing Lines of Communication

Communicating to people throughout your partnership hierarchy is very important. In the math professional-development group, a top-level person in one of the partner organizations was only vaguely aware that a partnership proposal was being developed. Upon seeing the work begin, and realizing he was almost entirely out of the loop, he reacted with frustration. Only after some negative interactions with members of the other partner organizations was he brought more fully into the communications loop. In contrast, the leaders of the science professional-development group continuously provided information to, and when necessary consulted with, everyone in the district science network. These messages and interactions left people throughout this network feeling respected and valued. By the time the working group was done with its tasks, its approach to professional development had been integrated into standard practice in the district.

## Message Framing

It matters how you frame your messages. Frames are cues that individuals use to categorize incoming information rapidly. Thus, frames efficiently assign meaning to particular events or occurrences (Goffman, 1974). The concept of framing is widely used in advertising and political communications; research in these areas highlights how framing can be used to make messages "sticky," or memorable, and to connect with specific audiences at an emotional level. For example, Nisbet and Mooney (2007) advocate that scientists pay attention to framing when they write for the public, and that they understand that topics such as climate change are at least as much about perception and politics as about scientific evidence. Partnership leaders should consider these issues when producing messages for different partnership stakeholders, particularly those in the trenches. It is all too common for top-level leaders to design a partnership without consulting with the staff who will ultimately implement it.

Research on framing in social movements and educational leadership reveals the potency of problem framing in reaching and motivating particular groups. For example, Cynthia Coburn found that school leaders play an important role in influencing how a reform message is ultimately interpreted and accepted (or not) by teachers (Coburn, 2001). Messages can be framed in ways that motivate people to take action, so spend some time drafting messages and test the drafts with working group members who best understand the local setting. When conveying important communications, you should remind your audience of the problem on which the partnership is focused, why you are seeking to address this problem now, and why your selected strategy is right for the situation. Each message should be framed in terms of your knowledge of the groups' cultural models and of the groups' current concerns pertaining to the problem. For example, if parents or the school board are dissatisfied with a new curriculum supported by the partnership, when communicating with them, make sure you convey a solid grasp of their concerns and that you have taken steps to address them. Far too many initiatives fail due to weak message framing. School leaders everywhere struggle with getting professional-development ideas past the initial presentation and training phases to the point of getting teacher buy-in at the classroom implementation level. All too often, in leaders' excitement to present what they see as a great idea, they forget to consider the cultural models and frames of mind of those for whom the message is intended. Is this great idea really something the intended beneficiaries want? Will it fill a need or solve a problem they think they have? If not, it won't work; reframing the message will increase the chance that the audience will accept the message.

## Chapter Summary

**Core Idea:** The work that partnership working groups engage in must be tailored to the unique needs and conditions of local stakeholders. These include the current workplace realities and constraints that teachers, faculty, staff, and administrators face on a day-to-day basis. Understanding the task environment will allow you to identify the leverage points with the most potential for effecting change and the appropriate type of intervention for your particular task environment.

### *Understand the Task Environment*

- Take the time to understand the local environment. This will convey to local stakeholders that you place a high value on getting to know local issues and personalities.
- Identify a key informant to help you understand the task environment; this person will point out important characteristics of the school, district, or IHE that you might miss because you are an outsider.

- Pay careful attention to the broader context in which a particular school or university operates, including state or local politics, economic conditions, and local cultural dynamics.
- Learn about past and current reform efforts at the location your partnership is targeting. Identify both successful and unsuccessful efforts that people will remember and that will color their view of your efforts.
- Use this information to help identify the most authentic, meaningful, and effective strategies and tasks for your partnership.

### Select a Leverage Point

- Identify a structural level or individual in the local hierarchy where you can target your work to have the greatest leverage.
- Determine an explicit strategy, either top-down (i.e., administrator-led), middle-out (i.e., midlevel administrator–led), or bottom-up (i.e., teacher- or faculty-led).

### Identify the Right Type of Intervention

- Consider the nature of the problem, your partnership's goals and objectives, and local conditions when designing your programs or interventions. If your problem is adaptive, you should choose an intervention *strategy*, and not focus exclusively on a specific type of intervention.

### Build Bridges to All Levels of the Local Partner Organization

- Carefully frame and sell your partnership to local constituents. Your message may differ depending on the level of the particular stakeholder group.

## Bibliographic Note

As noted earlier, we do not give guidance on implementing specific types of programs or interventions. Instead, our focus is akin to that of scholars such as Fullan (2001), who emphasize that reform efforts must be tailored to local conditions. Our perspective is anthropological, and we recommend Agar (1996) as an excellent guide for conducting ethnography. For a cautionary note on using ethnographic methods in education, see Wolcott (1997). See Tushnet (1993) for guidance on what local attributes you should take into consideration when designing your partnership as well as other useful recommendations.

*How People Learn: Brain, Mind, Experience, and School* by the National Research Council (2000) includes an excellent introduction to the learning sciences and the importance of authentic tasks in the learning process. For an introduction to research on professional-development schools, see R. W. Clark (1999a). For research on reform implementation and the role of local adaptation, see the review by Spillane, Reiser, and Reimer (2002). See Coburn (2001) for a discussion of how message framing unfolds at a single school site. For discussions of message framing, see Nisbet and Mooney (2007) (message control in science) and Heath and Heath (2007) (making ideas stick for any audience).

# 9

# DEVELOPING AND MANAGING
# WORKING GROUPS

Once you have identified the best strategies with which to realize your partnership's goals, it is time to put in place the teams, or working groups, that will implement the day-to-day operations that comprise partnership work. However, designing and managing working groups is not a simple task, and in this chapter we provide guidelines for effective management based on our study and the research literature. We define a *working group* as a set of individuals that (1) is responsible for accomplishing one or more tasks that are intended to help achieve one or more of a partnership's goals, (2) has at least two members who represent different organizations (or administrative units within the same organization), and (3) meets at least three times. Most partnerships have more than one working group, each with its own unique tasks, members, and characteristics. As a result each working group, like the overarching partnership to which it belongs, will need to identify the most appropriate organizational structure, administrative policies, and leadership arrangements.

The first part of the chapter provides general guidelines for designing and managing working groups with special attention to the most critical aspects of group operations that you should consider up front. Furthermore, since different partnership types will have different demands and require different management approaches, in the second part of the chapter we provide additional guidelines that apply to collaborative partnerships, as they present a unique set of administrative considerations and issues.

## Guidelines for All Working Groups

We have identified several guidelines for developing and managing working groups that, independent of their organizational structure, will help them function effectively and achieve their goals. These guidelines should be attended to in the order that best suits the particular group.

## Keep in Mind the Stage of Group Formation

As we noted in the introduction to this book, Tuckman and Jensen's (1977) stages-of-group-development framework can help you identify the evolutionary stage of a group within your partnership and the needs or considerations pertaining to that particular stage. For your convenience, we restate these stages:

- forming (individuals meet and get to know one another);
- storming (different ideas are considered and debated);
- norming (group members adjust behavior and agree on rules and procedures);
- performing (group members become interdependent and the group functions well); and
- adjourning (the group activities conclude).

Groups at each stage may require different types of resources and management. For instance, the UDEP science professional-development group used the stages-of-development framework to help group members make sense of the working group overall and to plan how to form and manage smaller subgroups. The leader kept this framework and its implications in mind as she considered when to form new subgroups and how their development, particularly during the turbulent forming and storming stages, would affect the overarching larger group and other subgroups running parallel with them. Her view was that it would be too challenging to have more than one subgroup storming at one time. Likewise, she determined that she and her coleader did not have the time and resources to help bring several groups to the performing stage at the same time. So she planned to initiate subgroups in sequence and ended up with several groups operating at the norming and performing stages.

## Obtain the Necessary Resources

As we noted in chapter 2, resources include not only material resources such as money and materials but also human (i.e., skills and knowledge) and social (i.e., networks) resources. Each of these is a crucial ingredient for supporting the people working in your partnership. Thus, one of the first steps in launching a partnership working group is for leaders to obtain the resources their group needs to undertake its tasks.

## Material Resources

Partnership work tends to be material resource intensive. In 1988, Sirotnik and Goodlad noted the disparity between, on one hand, the rhetoric about partnerships and their expected achievements, and, on the other, the financial commitments actually made to partnerships. While recent increases in partnership funding work may have narrowed this gap, questions remain about whether the expectations for partnership outcomes are commensurate with both funding levels and timelines. In light of these concerns be sure the tasks you assign to a working group are commensurate with the available resources. If you consistently expect more than the resources can support, participants might become frustrated and burn out. Also, make sure that group members have adequate administrative support and easy access to the materials they need, whether they are supplies, working space, travel money, or stipends. Also pay careful attention to ensuring that these resources are provided to staff and others on a timely basis. The UDEP partnership learned this lesson the hard way, when stipends to participating K–12 teachers in a summer workshop were delayed. This administrative glitch disrupted the program and did not reflect well on the partnership as a whole.

## Human Resources

Human resources are attributes of individuals, such as skills, knowledge, expertise, and time. Organizations draw on the human resources of their own staff and of people outside the organization to meet their goals. Similarly, it would also be necessary to identify what types of human resources are necessary to accomplish your working group's tasks. For example, a professional-development program for middle-school teachers may require staff with knowledge of math content, math standards for that grade level, and the types of classroom experiences teachers typically need. Once you've identified the types of human resources you need, recruit people who have the desired qualifications. Look in-house, use networks, or seek out individuals with specific skill sets.

Once a group is up and running, it might be necessary to move people around, as roles evolve and as individual talents and interests become clearer (Tushnet, 1993). In addition to recruiting people with the needed expertise, be sure to include among your selection criteria the abilities to cross organizational boundaries and communicate effectively. Whenever possible, include people who understand and represent the stakeholders who should benefit from the group's work. Once you have engaged individuals as group members, make sure they have the training they need to do the expected work. For instance, the science professional-development group regularly used consensus-based decision making, so participants were trained in this collaborative process.

An important human resource is the professional time of your working group members. The professional time of some members may be funded by partnership grants. In the case of big grants, a few individuals, such as project managers, are actually employees of the partnership. For almost all grants, some of the time of some people in each partner organization is "bought" with the grant funds. The time of others is provided by their home organizations. For example, home organization managers may agree to relieve employees of some responsibilities so they can devote time to the partnership. Examples include K–12 professional-development staff who perform part of their core responsibility for a partnership, or IHE faculty who participate in professional-development workshops to fulfill the service element of their roles. Last, and perhaps most common, members devote time to partnerships on top of their regular responsibilities. This experience is common even for individuals who have part of their time released or bought out, because the time the partnership demands substantially exceeds the released time. In these cases, partnership work often comes to be associated with stress and burnout.

Use management strategies to minimize this problem. Note the commitment level of each person, particularly that of leaders who are likely to be the most overcommitted and try to reduce their responsibilities and tasks. In UDEP, some leaders attempted to participate in several working groups while also tending to roles in their home organizations. These individuals often became bottlenecks for their groups' efforts and tended to experience burnout more quickly than others. Moreover, in collaborative partnerships, the goal of dispersing leadership is impeded when just a few individuals take the leadership roles in many groups. To prevent this from happening, empower many individuals as group leaders and discourage overcommitment. As for time management, a useful principle is that the work needs to fit the time available. In other words, treat the reality of limited staff time as an opportunity to focus your priorities and identify which activities are truly essential and which are not (Hamm, 2006). A vital strategy is to operate in an efficient, well-organized manner, thus optimizing the value of the staff time you have. A good communication system and effective administrative processes are crucial for optimizing the use of working group members' time.

> **Partnership Action Point:** Take care that your project staff do not have competing time commitments. Burnout is common in partnership work as people take on projects in addition to their everyday responsibilities.

## Consider Support Systems

Instead of viewing resources as a one-time infusion of funds and staffing into a working group, think of them as a long-term support system and safety net. Such a support system can take many forms, including partnership leaders who are available to provide feedback to group leaders and participants, or it can be the provision of additional resources as the work unfolds. This is especially important in situations in which dramatic change or reform is being attempted. It is important to understand that "the greater the change expected of the participant, the more individualized and intense the technical support and content assistance should be" (Tushnet, 1993, p. 22). Problems will arise, people will forget how to do things, and the entire working group may unexpectedly get off track, or become frustrated when things don't go as planned. Individuals or groups within partner schools, districts, or IHEs may pose barriers to change, and people engaged in partnership work may need assistance in overcoming the inertia or outright resistance they encounter. If support systems are already in place, it will be easy for participants to seek help rather than just give up. Change is difficult, and most people think of themselves as busy or overworked. When faced with adversity, the easiest path is often back to what was done before. Support systems, therefore, need to be easily accessible and nonthreatening.

## Arrange for a Leader Who Is an Effective Manager

The people you ask to manage working groups not only should be capable boundary crossers but also should be skilled managers. Certain managerial practices and skills should be in your leaders' tool kits.

### Establish Clear Procedures and Policies

One of the most effective actions working group managers can take is to provide structure and a clear direction for their group. Groups that lack structure or direction tend to make poor use of participants' time and other resources. Because working groups in partnerships usually are new creations, each requires, in miniature, the same organizational elements of the larger partnership—goals and objectives, a governance system, communication protocols, and specific tasks, among others—all of which a manager must establish for a functional group.

### Foster Progressive Communications Among Group Members

Managers need to establish communication systems for the groups they oversee, instead of assuming that e-mail and infrequent meetings will suffice. The experiences of the preservice math group demonstrated how a lack of protocols for communication limited the development of trust and the productivity of meetings. The group started out with a basic agenda for how to revise a sequence of preservice courses at the university but did not clarify the group's goals, objectives, or management protocols. In particular, there was no discussion of how meetings would proceed, such as who would set agendas and chair the discussions. The lack of communication protocols allowed regressive interactions to emerge. The leader, a mathematics faculty member who did not have a strong knowledge of mathematics education or the realities of the K–12 classroom, controlled the direction of the discussion and gave priority to the opinions of other math faculty. As a result, the math education faculty and K–12 representatives felt relegated to playing second fiddle to the IHE faculty. In interviews, group members expressed resentment, citing a lack of open dialogue and a tendency for members to push their own agendas in an effort to resist control by the dominant leader.

In contrast, the leaders of the science professional-development group paid careful attention to communication procedures and established a very inclusive approach to meetings and planning sessions. They created a level playing field where all members had an equal say in developing guides for use during professional-development implementation. Although fostering an atmosphere of open and honest communication may look easy, it requires effort and skill on the part of group leaders: they need to set clear ground rules for debate and discussion and actively guide cross-cultural and cross-organizational interactions so they proceed in a progressive manner. The outcome, however, is worth the effort. The science professional-development group developed a common vision (indeed, it became an affinity group), and its products were well received precisely because they were shaped by input from the individuals who would be affected most.

## Specify Roles and Responsibilities

One of the key findings from our analysis of the UDEP partnership is the importance of clearly specifying roles and responsibilities for working group members. Unless a leader or manager does this, participants will not be clear about what they should be doing or about the ultimate goals of their group, and they are likely to remain unconvinced that committing precious time and energy to the effort is worthwhile. In particular, we found that managers should state clear goals and tasks for individual group members, clarify role expectations, and celebrate group successes as they happen as a way to mark the group's progress.

### State Clear Goals and Tasks for Group Members

A working group's goals and specific tasks must be stated clearly, and time-lines and benchmarks should be established. In cases in which the tasks involve more creative or emergent work, such as adaptive challenges, it is important to provide the working group with at least a vision of what the final product might be. Examples include developing a new policy or curric-ulum; in such situations, the intended outcome is undetermined at the beginning. A group is better able to see the value of its work if goals are clear, because the group will know what it is aiming for. If you are embed-ding formative evaluation processes into the work, you will be able to assess progress toward the goals and identify what is working and what is not so you can adjust and adapt as necessary.

Groups also tend to function much more effectively if their task involves producing a tangible product (e.g., a syllabus, a policy, a teaching guide, or an assessment tool) that one or more of the partner organizations will use. In these situations, members are far more likely to become deeply engaged, because the product is a symbolic and actual focal point for the work. Tangi-ble products also are signs of productivity that stakeholders (including fund-ers) understand. As noted previously, it is important to make sure that working group members have enough time for their work. Timelines help structure tasks and ensure that the work unfolds in a way that permits coor-dination of the efforts of several people working on different elements of the task. Clearly delineated and measurable objectives are important so the group as a whole understands whether key tasks are being accomplished and so staff can step back occasionally and appraise their progress honestly. That said, managers cannot assume that, by establishing objectives, their work is done; they should actively monitor individual and group progress.

### Clarify Role Expectations

Role and performance expectations are key aspects of organizational life. They are even more important in work settings in which participants must cross cultural or organizational boundaries. Effective working group managers ensure that all participants understand not only the goals of the group but also what roles each participant plays (e.g., product developer, meeting facilitator). By clarifying role expectations, you will also increase individuals' accountability to the group. For instance, the leader of the science professional-development group worked to ensure that all members of the professional-development group understood their role well enough that they knew their importance, and felt accountable, to the entire group. In this way, each participant knew how his or her role enabled the entire group to achieve its goals.

*Celebrate Success*

Partnership work tends to be very demanding and time-consuming, and it is tempting to keep your nose to the grindstone at all times. Working group managers should celebrate the successes of the group, however small they may seem. Accomplishments such as meeting deadlines, delivering a high-quality product, or securing a new grant or contract should be marked by some sort of public declaration or observance. Although it is not necessarily easy for managers to create a culture for a group, by marking accomplishments formally, leaders can help establish a shared identity and set of expectations for the collective.

## Additional Guidelines for Collaborative Working Groups

Partnership groups designed to operate in a collaborative manner need to establish a higher level of interdependence than do coordinated or limited groups. It is challenging to accomplish this with group members who come from different partner organizations and have different expertise and perspectives. Yet, the closer your partnership is to the collaborative end of the partnership typology (see chapter 5), the greater the opportunity to produce synergistic knowledge and products, group identity, and enduring networks. In short, collaborative working groups have the potential to create new affinity groups, by which we mean groups of practitioners who share common tasks, language or jargon, social norms, and a collective identity. Here we offer several additional guidelines to help managers of collaborative working groups.

### Integrate Members From Different Affinity Groups

For many tasks, and especially for adaptive challenges, diverse expertise is required. For example, a partnership may bring together IHE faculty with content expertise and K–12 teachers with pedagogical expertise to create new curricula. Leaders need to remember that these diverse members come from different affinity groups in their home organizations and bring with them their communities' cultural models (e.g., models pertaining to theories of action, collaboration, and task implementation). When exploring models for theories of action, consider how the preexisting group thinks the problem can best be addressed and what the implications are for the work. Regarding cultural models pertaining to collaboration, ask how members of the partner affinity groups collaborate and what they believe about collaboration. Should tasks be planned and implemented collectively or by partner-based sub-groups? With respect to task implementation, determine whether the members of preexisting groups are used to a hierarchical delegation of tasks, and if so, whether the partnership should adopt that.

Some of these cultural models may be fairly rigid or nonnegotiable. Successful communication and cross-organizational work will depend on how you identify and share such knowledge in your 3rd-space group. This is a complex process for a boundary-spanning group. It involves the negotiation of multiple domains of knowledge, by actors who possess at best a partial understanding of domains other than their own. In a study of a school-university partnership, leaders without local knowledge could not provide intellectual stimulation and inspirational vision to the project staff (Houck, Cohn, & Cohn, 2004). Because there were no boundary-crosser leaders who could synergize across groups, leaders and staff formed cliques, and pockets of influence developed. It is up to the leaders of the partnership as a whole, and of individual working groups, to integrate different affinity groups to capitalize on the synergies available in a collaborative partnership.

### Encourage Collaboration and Synergy

It is also necessary to create opportunities for face-to-face interaction to foster the development of an affinity group. Create a safe environment where members feel comfortable sharing and discussing varying viewpoints. Establish this kind of environment as early as possible, because it provides the grounds on which to nurture trust and common vision. One UDEP science professional-development group member described a strategy the group leaders used to encourage a safe environment: they structured tasks so all members participated as learners rather than as experts trying to outshine one another. This helped establish trust and a collaborative atmosphere and made it easier to work toward common goals. One group member expressed appreciation that the group's meetings were open environments focused

more on underlying ideas than on specific content. As a result, many participants felt their ideas were valid, which in turn led to development of strong
working groups built on relational trust. One participant noted, "It wasn't
the curricular units that we were producing that were the most powerful
thing. It was really the collaboration that was resulting from doing this product development work together that was the most powerful."

*Co-Construction and Co-Teaching as a Strategy*

One strategy for encouraging collaboration and synergy is to engage individuals in work that requires close, personal interactions. Examples may include
the joint creation of specific artifacts such as a new instructional unit or co-
teaching a professional-development workshop. By co-teaching, we mean
instructors sharing the responsibility for teaching a single group of students
at the same time. For example, Houck et al. (2004) studied an effort to
develop summer professional development for first- and second-grade teachers in which two teachers and one university faculty collaborated in planning
and then teaching a course on literacy. The teachers and faculty learned from
one another when planning the course, with the K–12 staff emphasizing
best practices in teaching reading based on their experience, and the faculty
emphasizing adult learning theory as it informed the delivery of the content.
Although co-teaching can go badly, when done right, this strategy has strong
positive outcomes. For example, in the IDEP partnership, when faculty from
math and math education worked together to design and co-teach a course
for preservice elementary teachers, they saw up close for the first time how
the other discipline thought about and approached teaching.

In addition, one of the core strategies of the science professional-development group was the construction of new science-immersion units. This
strategy hinged on bringing STEM and education faculty, K–12 teachers and
teacher-leaders, and professional-development specialists together to create
the immersion units collaboratively. These groups worked together to co-
teach the units during the summer workshops for K–12 teachers, which
required an intense amount of interaction among individuals from different
professional and disciplinary backgrounds. This strategy paid off, resulting
in perhaps the most successful attempt at forging an affinity group in the
UDEP partnership. One participant noted, "As we worked on the facilitation guides, there was a real cohesion between teachers, administrators, university faculty, professional developers, and district science leadership—all
of us began to think in the same way and really began to walk the walk

about collaboration and coherence, and that was powerful." The collaborative work enabled close interactions among different participants, and relationships slowly began to emerge as people's trust in one another's competence and respect for different areas of expertise grew. Of particular significance was that university faculty had to learn to teach differently; in the process they discovered they had things to gain from, not just things to give to, the partnership. In this case, the willingness of all participants to learn from one another was a watershed for the group.

*The Importance of Co-Constructed Products*

Another centerpiece of the science professional-development group's effort to create an effective working group was to focus on developing a tangible product that represented the working group's shared efforts. The facilitation guide that the group developed inspired the group and focused its attention on an object that served multiple parties' needs. A co-constructed document, policy, or curriculum is the crystallization of multiple minds and areas of expertise and demonstrates to the group that created it what is possible when different people's skills synergize to advance teaching and learning. In short, joint construction of a product can lead to the creation of a new cultural model for a group and physically exemplify that model. These products need not be physical objects (e.g., a facilitation guide, classroom laboratory items); they may be policies and procedures that shape behavior and practice (Halverson, 2003). The point is that the product be sufficiently tangible to represent the collaborative work of the members and thus serve as a powerful symbol of the shared experience.

---

**Partnership Action Point:** Consider having your working group members engage in the construction of a new product or policy; such work can lead to the formation of a strong collective identity.

---

## Dealing Proactively With Conflict and Tension Facilitates Learning and Creativity

One of the most widely accepted ingredients for cross-organizational partnership success is a common vision. Having a collective vision and sense of purpose helps establish a road map for all participants to follow and reminds the group's members why they are taking the risks of partnership in the first place. Establishing such a vision entails developing a common vocabulary in which all participants understand key terms in the same way. The meaning of core terms such as "curriculum" or "professional development" may seem obvious, but it is precisely these types of ubiquitous terms that may mean different things to people from different groups. That said, creating a common vision is not about smoothing out all differences between different groups. Some differences cannot and should not be resolved but, instead, should be considered potential areas for learning and growth. Thus, while partnerships need a certain amount of congruence, persistent differences among partners should be appreciated as an opportunity to capitalize on diverse areas of expertise and insight.

In addition, some sort of conflict or unforeseen change probably will take place in your partnership (see chapter 10). For instance, personnel changes are exceptionally common in education, particularly in the K–12 sector. Superintendent turnover is likely to occur and can jeopardize the entire partnership, because a change at the helm sometimes results in a large turnover among staff, changes in strategy (e.g., curricular, organizational), and shifting power dynamics. Over the course of the UDEP partnership, two different changes in superintendents took place in the large urban district in which the science professional-development group worked. The group managed to weather the storm by keeping key individuals in place, but the shifting playing field of district politics and decisions made the outcomes for this group less certain. In such circumstances, a leader must demonstrate adaptive expertise and continually be on the lookout for creative ways to work with and around these challenges.

## *Be Flexible*

Few, if any, partnerships get collaborative work and effective coordination right the first time. Partnership leaders must continually monitor progress as well as local needs and other contextual factors. For example, the science professional-development group originally set out to identify preexisting inquiry-based curriculum units that were inexpensive to implement and had solid records. The group initially identified two such units but soon realized that these did not serve the district's needs. Hence the group needed to change course. If your partnership is tackling an adaptive challenge, you will also need to be flexible and allow for evolution of the specific working groups that are actually implementing the work of the partnership. As we mentioned earlier, the philosophy of flexibility the designers of the Condor distributed-computing project followed is worth considering. These features included letting communities grow naturally, leaving group leaders and participants in control, planning without being picky, and lending and borrowing expertise and knowledge (Thain, Tannenbaum, & Livny, 2005).

A flexible stance is important when a collaborative working group needs to change course. Although a group leader may believe the members are proceeding down the wrong path, and may need to intervene eventually, he or she should remember that letting groups explore their own path has some benefits. One participant said, "Sometimes it's a good strategy to let people follow a path you suspect won't work because (a) it may work, and (b) they'll end up at a different place where they're ready to consider a different strategy." The goals may not change, but the tactics to reach the goals probably will shift with circumstances. For instance, the science professional-development group had been working on inquiry-based curriculum units when the district decided to adopt a comprehensive elementary curriculum for science that was not aligned well with an inquiry approach. But the group recognized the hand it had been dealt and decided to provide professional development to teachers that was a hybrid model of teaching the new curriculum in the same way the units they had been working on were taught. Thus, the group was able to take the change in stride and adapt it to the group's goals. This allowed everyone to work together, gain ownership of the work, and create a product that met the needs of the district.

> **Partnership Action Point:** Adopt a flexible approach to working group management. Let communities and working groups grow naturally, leave group leaders and participants in control, plan without being picky, and lend and borrow expertise and knowledge.

## Chapter Summary

> **Core Idea:** Effective working groups require adequate resources and flexible leadership. Groups in collaborative partnerships are particularly challenging to manage because they bring together individuals from disparate backgrounds with different cultural models. Leaders of these groups will need to integrate the group members' different cultural models, use strategies (e.g., co-constructing new artifacts, co-teaching) that encourage collaboration, and use conflict as a source of creativity.

### Guidelines for All Working Groups

- Consider the stage of group formation (e.g., forming, storming) when managing a working group.
- Obtain the necessary material and human resources to perform the tasks delegated to each working group adequately.
- Establish support systems, so group leaders and participants have other people and resources to call on in times of change or conflict.
- Select working group leaders who are effective managers. These individuals should be able to establish clear group procedures and policies, state tasks clearly, provide feasible timelines and develop benchmarks, and clarify role expectations.
- Specify key goals and tasks of the group as well as each participant's specific roles and responsibilities.

### Guidelines for Collaborative Working Groups

- Integrate different affinity groups to accomplish common tasks. Leaders must take the time to understand the cultural models that motivate each participant and address the implications of these models for the tasks at hand.
- Encourage collaboration and synergy through co-construction of new products (e.g., curricula) or engaging participants in co-teaching activities.
- Deal proactively with conflict and tension.
- Be flexible in the face of new conditions or evidence that the current direction is not appropriate or effective.

## Bibliographic Note

For a discussion of the resources required to conduct education partnerships, see Houck et al. (2004) and Sirotnik and Goodlad (1988). Also see the Houck et al. (2004) book *Partnering to Lead Educational Renewal* for the anecdote about the leader who did not have strong experience with K–12 schools. For a discussion of the role of organizational routines and structures in shaping behavior, see Halverson (2003). See Gray (1989) for the importance of establishing a common vision and collective identity when conducting collaborative work. For a discussion of the potential of creative abrasion, see Seely Brown and Duguid (2002). Hamm (2006) provides a compelling account of leadership communications that some UDEP participants found helpful.

# IO

# THE KEY ROLES OF TRUST
# AND MANAGING CONFLICT

Both trust and conflict play central roles in partnerships. Conflict and disagreement are inevitable in the 3rd space, as people from different organizations, disciplines, and backgrounds must work together to address complex problems that invariably will elicit competing strategies and interpretations about the best course of action. A strong foundation of trust among different individuals and groups can help mitigate the effects of conflict and tensions, while also laying the ground work for protective working relationships. However, if conflict is left undetected or is handled poorly, it can erode trust and lead to a negative cycle of further conflict and eventual partnership failure. In contrast, when conflict is managed through respectful and thoughtful interactions, a positive cycle of increasing trust and productivity tends to prevail.

You may have experienced this dynamic between conflict and trust. We observed it in all of the UDEP working groups. In a common scenario, classroom teachers reported that when they began working with particular university faculty they felt vulnerable and intimidated: How would these people, many of whom had much more knowledge of the disciplinary content, treat them? Would these faculty recognize that the teachers, in turn, have experience and knowledge that everyone needs to enable students to learn math and science? As the teachers learned through experience that these faculty treated them with respect and wanted to benefit from their views and knowledge, they began to feel comfortable enough to challenge and critique the faculty and to be challenged and critiqued in return. They had moved into the positive cycle of trust, creative abrasion, and productivity. A leader's role is to help establish a safe atmosphere in which engaging in creative conflict is part of a group's regular routines. In this chapter we focus first on the dynamics of trust and how to develop trust in partnerships. We then turn to the nature of conflict and how to manage it to move a partnership into a positive cycle of increasing trust and productivity.

## Dynamics of Trust in Partnerships

Where there is no trust, there is no partnership. Trust is needed in limited partnerships that use top-down governance models: partners working under even the most formal contractual arrangements require that the other partners consistently provide what is promised. Trust is a far more crucial factor in a coordinated partnership or in a collaborative partnership using a consensus-based governance model. Trust is what enables diverse members of working groups to agree to address challenging tasks (e.g., reforming science instruction in a large urban school district), take intellectual and even professional risks, and stick with the work despite intense demands on their time and the lack of certain success.

Rotter (1980) defines trust as "a generalized expectancy held by an individual that the word, promise, or statement of another individual can be relied upon" (p. 107). Central to trust is the concept of risk: can you trust that a partner will not act opportunistically in a way that harms you? Trust is willingness to assume that a partner will bear the vulnerability of this risk—to guard against the uncertainties and risks involved in sharing assets and power with another group. Trust is especially important in the forming stage, when each partner is attempting to determine whether the others are likely to be trustworthy. You probably should not proceed with potential partners who do not pass this initial vetting (see part one). That said, it is unrealistic to assume that you will establish substantial levels of trust in your first pre-partnership planning meeting. Trust is developed incrementally and over time. Even in situations in which prior embedded relationships have provided evidence of another group's ability to perform, any new venture carries with it a certain amount of risk.

> **Partnership Action Point:** Pay careful attention to nurturing trust among your partners. Trust will develop as partners begin to view one another as predictable, dependable, and operating in good faith.

According to Holmes and Rempel (1989), trust is developed in three steps. The first step is becoming convinced, based on behavioral evidence, that your potential partners are *predictable*. The second step is a willingness to view them as *dependable*. The last step is developing *faith* in the other partner, which entails an emotional security that the partner can be counted on to deliver on his or her promises over the long term. Trust is generated over time as partners develop confidence in one another's goodwill and effectiveness and begin to be able to anticipate one another's behavior. It is a particularly necessary ingredient in educational partnerships, where groups with longstanding tensions that may hold deeply entrenched stereotypes of one another come together in a collaborative work setting. As one UDEP participant noted, "At first we trusted each other just to hold up our own corner of the tent, but did not necessarily point out what should be done in each other's corners. As the roles and tasks melded, that enabled the opening up of more trust." In terms of creating trusting work environments, congruent expectations and shared visions for the work are a cumulative product of numerous interactions among individuals.

Satisfactory interactions, positive communication, and successful work forge the new friendships and social-psychological bonds needed for a successful collaborative partnership. It is unlikely that partners will develop a sense of trust and collective identity if they lack opportunities to engage in meaningful work that is at least partially successful. For example, when writing the grant that launched their partnership, top-level UDEP leaders did not seek substantial input from people who would be affected at the mid-level (e.g., department and center leaders and managers), let alone the ground level (teachers). In their efforts to win grant money in a compressed time frame, their focus was on big-picture selling points rather than on local needs. After the work began, it quickly became apparent that many mid- and ground-level people who would be directly affected were uninformed about the project and unprepared to work with the other organizations in the partnership. One of the partner organization's leaders belatedly recognized that these key leaders needed to be more integrated into the planning and decision making of partnership, but valuable opportunities had been lost and a certain degree of mistrust already had taken root.

## Strategies for Developing Trust

Trust management is about managing the risk and vulnerability inherent in the collaborative situation.

(Vangen & Huxham, 2003)

In this section, we outline some of the core components that contribute to high levels of trust within partnerships.

## Establish Predictability

Ambiguity, flux and unpredictability are common features of partnership work, but trust depends on feeling that you can accurately predict that a particular partner is capable of accomplishing a task or delivering a product on time. However, it can be difficult to develop this sense of predictability if people are not provided with opportunities to develop a clear track record, or if personnel changes are so frequent that you never know precisely who it is that you are working with. In light of these not uncommon challenges to predictability, we offer two strategies that can help you to develop a sense of certainty and predictability about your partners.

First, establish clear and specific expectations about what each partner will accomplish in the partnership, which provides them with the opportunity to successfully complete a task and for you to build confidence in their reliability. While specific tasks may evolve or remain ambiguous for periods of time, take care to "nail down" specific tasks for working groups and individuals, as people generally find it reassuring to know what is expected of them and what they can expect of others. Once these expectations are met (assuming they are), then the individual or group is on the road to becoming a predictable and dependable partner.

A second important strategy is to require, or at least strive to ensure, the stability of leadership. Regular turnover in key leadership positions can wreak havoc on group formation and establishing a sense of confidence and reliability that a group can perform effectively. As one participant in the science professional development group observed, "If the leadership had changed, we wouldn't be nearly as far along as we are now." The longevity and commitment of these leaders was vital to establishing the trust and confidence of working group members, which was a key ingredient in making this particular group so productive and effective. Thus, a leader can do much to establish a regular, consistent presence.

## Engage in Plenty of Face-to-Face Interaction

Trust develops through personal relationships as coworkers or colleagues experience work and life together. These bonds are formed through close, personal interactions. This is why several UDEP participants bemoaned the fact that some group members had few opportunities for face-to-face interactions, which would have enabled them to work, laugh, share conversation over a meal, and experience together the successes and failures of group work. Communicating exclusively by phone or e-mail is less effective for developing trust and a sense of collegiality.

## Create an Emotionally Safe Working Environment

A trusting working environment is one in which people feel safe to disagree with each other. When conflict and disagreement emerge, a leader should model good conflict management for the group by listening respectfully and fully, identifying and affirming the value of different cultural models, and diagnosing the problem as fairly and accurately as possible. Work to defuse emotions (humor and coffee breaks are useful for this), and encourage all participants to come up with creative ways to move forward.

## Engage the People Most Affected by the Partnership

Engage the personnel who will be most affected by the work, and ensure that their views are integrated into the design of the work. This trust-building strategy is particularly important in education; so many reforms and new initiatives have been imposed on faculty and classroom teachers that they are accustomed to saying, "This, too, shall pass." By engaging the personnel who are the target audience of the partnership, and obtaining their perspectives and opinions on the work, a leader takes an important step toward establishing an environment of respect and trust.

## Surface and Manage Power Dynamics

Power struggles are common in partnerships, and they erode trust, thus damaging partnership. Who gets to control the direction of the initiative and the resources? Is someone stepping on your turf? Is everyone getting the credit he or she deserves? It is important to address these concerns as soon as they appear and to agree on how to resolve them for the benefit of the whole. Mutual trust can develop even in situations in which one group is clearly dominant. In the not uncommon scenario in which structural power imbalances are present, acknowledge them and proceed to develop trust using the same strategies that work when power is balanced.

## Managing Conflict in Education Partnerships

Successful partnerships acknowledge and confront problems, using them as the opportunity to build relationships among parties.

(Tushnet, 1993)

Despite the ubiquity of conflict in educational organizations and partnerships, and the voluminous literature on conflict management and resolution, the topic is rarely addressed in educational partnership studies. Similarly, conflict-resolution procedures are not required in proposals for grant-funded partnership initiatives. The cost of launching a partnership without conflict-management skills and agreements is high. In this section we present some conflict-management principles and techniques that are relevant to partnership work and that lie outside the parameters of the established conflict-management processes within educational organizations, such as those found in union agreements and human resource policies.

## Diagnosing the Type and Nature of Conflict in Organizations

Conflicts can be diagnosed by who they effect and whether or not they are malevolent or benevolent. Owens (2001) provides a framework for diagnosing the types of conflict, each of which was evident in the UDEP partnership, and each of which we briefly describe here.

### Types of Conflict

*Intrapersonal conflict* happens within an individual and often is characterized by a desire to pursue two incompatible goals, which can lead to indecisiveness and stress. Such stress can compound the normal stresses associated with educational work, and intrapersonal conflict is especially likely to occur in partnerships. Boundary crossers, who are necessary for partnership operations, often experience this problem in what is known as "role conflict." As boundary crossers interact with people from different groups and backgrounds, each of whom has expectations about the boundary crosser's behavior and activities, the boundary crosser is likely to experience conflicting expectations about how to fulfill his or her role. Role conflict not only is harmful to the individuals who experience it, but also to the partnership, which is affected by the stress these leaders experience.

More obvious and visible is *interpersonal conflict*, which takes place between two or more individuals. This type of conflict may stem from a desire to pursue divergent, incompatible goals or from incompatible personalities or communication styles. Whatever the cause, these conflicts can be debilitating, because it is often hard for participants to depersonalize a situation. In our study of the UDEP project, we discovered that two of the three top leaders had conflicts with each other, thereby inhibiting the efficacy of the entire project.

*Intragroup conflict* often erupts within a group or an organization. In partnerships, this commonly takes one of two forms. First, different units such as departments or subcultures within schools or universities may be in conflict. Second, conflict may emerge among representatives from different units who participate in a newly formed partnership working group. When this type of conflict emerges within a working group, do not ignore it and hope it will go away. It probably will only get worse, so give it immediate attention. Given the different and often divergent cultural environments from which most groups come, a partnership is also ripe territory for *intergroup conflict*. In fact, the stereotypes that some educators ascribe to their counterparts in the K–12 or higher education sector or in different disciplines make such conflict likely and, thus, important to anticipate and defuse. In other cases, different organizations may simply have divergent, incompatible goals and theories of action. This type of conflict can also occur within organizations, as different departments or administrative units develop enmity and disagreements.

## Nature of Conflict

Once you've identified what type of conflict you're dealing with, you should determine whether the conflict is benevolent or malevolent. Kenneth Boulding (1962) distinguishes between *malevolent hostility*, which seeks to hurt the position of another individual or group with no regard for the well-being of the victim or consequences for the attacker, and *benevolent* hostility, which seeks to improve the position of the attacker. Owens (2001) makes a distinction between hostility and conflict: hostility is characterized by "nefarious attacks" (p. 307). Attributes of nefarious attacks include (1) a focus on people, not issues; (2) use of hateful language; (3) use of dogmatic statements rather than questions; (4) maintenance of fixed views regardless of new information or argument; and (5) use of emotional terms. When this kind of behavior is present, red flags should go up, as the trust you have attempted to build is at great risk. You should try to avoid or minimize malevolent or hostile types of conflict, as these can wreak havoc on a partnership.

Identifying the type and nature of conflict will help you develop and implement conflict-management strategies.

## Strategies for Managing Conflict

Some degree of conflict or tension is inevitable in partnership work, and it is the responsibility of the leaders of the partnership as a whole or of individual working groups to address the conflict in a proactive and progressive manner. In this section we review some of the more productive methods for dealing with organizational conflict, including building a foundation of trust and viewing conflict as opportunity.

### Attempt to Restore a Modicum of Trust

If serious conflict arises, you must try to respond quickly, respectfully, and fairly. If you don't, the trust you are trying to foster might be damaged permanently. Make clear that behavior that disparages, thoughtlessly or arrogantly overrides, or marginalizes group members is not acceptable. If you are identified, through partner membership or disciplinary affiliation, with one of the people involved in the conflict, be sure to put aside your own ego and agenda. Everyone in the group will pay attention to whether you can do this and whether you can guide the group proactively through the conflict. In short, act to create an environment in which all participants feel that their expertise is respected and their contributions are needed.

### View Conflict as Opportunity

The most effective overall conflict-management strategy is to view conflict as opportunity. Achieving success is less about whether disagreements occur than it is about how they are managed. An organization or a partnership that can deal effectively with conflict can learn from it. Conflict and disruption also serve a positive purpose by providing partnerships with opportunities for creative abrasion, collective problem solving, and the generation of renewed organizational and individual relations. As Tushnet (1993) says, "Successful partnerships acknowledge and confront problems, using them as the opportunity to build relationships among partners" (p. xi). If at all possible, try to view problems as stimulating challenges, as opportunities to reexamine policies and reconsider the direction of a partnership activity or the partnership's global goals. Successful partnerships are organizations that learn from mistakes, are open to change, and respond proactively to challenges and conflicts (Senge, 1994). You can learn from mistakes, and you need to be open to change. Consider each conflict to be an opportunity to reflect on your conflict-management processes.

---

**Partnership Action Point:** Make your partnership a problem-finding organization by using your evaluation data to identify conflicts and other problems and address them quickly.

---

Another way to implement the conflict-as-opportunity strategy is to design your partnership as a problem-finding organization that continually seeks to identify problems and address them head-on before they can wreak havoc. This task will be easier if a formative evaluation system has been established within the partnership, so that problems on the ground can be identified quickly and communicated to the leadership. Such a diagnostic assessment system should be established at the outset of a partnership.

### Use Leadership Techniques

Leaders can address conflicts and disruptions by changing the composition of groups. This may entail reassigning staff whose presence is disruptive or who are not being team players. Jim Collins (2001) made this a key principle in his book *Good to Great*, in which he called for ensuring that leaders "get the right people on the bus" (p. 41).

In cases where there is known tension or outright hostility between groups, one technique is for one group member to establish a friendly one-on-one relationship with a member of the other group. In our study, an education faculty member recognized the depth of the hostility between her department and the math department and made a concerted effort to establish a working relationship with one of the pricklier faculty members. She invited him to observe her classes, asked for his opinion, and held private discussions with him, thereby developing the trust necessary to discuss what she viewed as his misconceptions. In fact, her commitment to building a relationship enabled them to trust each other enough to collaborate on teaching a course. Finally, given the strong points of view and emotions at play in partnerships, it can be easy to take differences of opinion personally and allow conversation to devolve into acrimony. Try to see all disagreements as professional, not personal.

### Use Procedural Techniques

Various procedures and techniques are available for dealing with conflict in partnerships. Some of these may involve legal affairs offices or other official venues within partner organizations, but others can be used by partnership leaders on their own.

### Keep Formal and Informal Lines of Communication Open

Conflicts cannot be identified or resolved without consistent, open communication. Shutting down in the face of disagreement or avoiding a problem completely will only allow the conflict to become harmful to the partnership.

Put in place procedures that ensure that the right people are communicating frequently enough and in effective ways—such as face-to-face—in both well-designed formal meetings and in less-formal settings. If people are talking behind other people's backs, your contact architecture needs improvement.

### Establish Administrative Structures for Handling Conflict

The 3rd space of partnerships does not come with a human resources department to which you can direct your concerns or grievances. Because most partnerships lack a clear chain of command and have murkier roles and responsibilities, it is more difficult to find the "right" person to handle a given conflict than it is in established organizations. Distinguish your partnership from most others by establishing adequate structures and procedures for handling conflict. In UDEP, there was no such structure. The lack of structure, coupled with unclear leadership and roles, led to situations in which neutral individuals became bogged down in other participants' disagreements.

### Enlist Mediators

As a last resort, you should consider enlisting third-party mediators, who may succeed in helping conflicting parties find a common ground and an acceptable resolution to a dispute. A mediator should not be a member of one of the groups involved in the conflict. Furthermore, all parties must be open to mediation and realize that it is necessary for the group to progress. Thus, some conflict is often necessary before mediation is viewed as an option.

### Separate When Necessary

In some cases, it will be in the best interests of all partners to dissolve the partnership before it has run its intended course. The cause may be an egregious violation such as financial impropriety, or partners simply might decide that the costs outweigh the benefits. Collaboration makes sense only as long as the partners can satisfy one another's differing interests without hurting themselves. As Lee Teitel (1998) observed about professional-development partnerships, breakdowns and reconfigurations of partnerships are common, and in some cases partners may find it necessary to divorce themselves completely from the arrangement. The decision to separate is typically not sudden, and in the case we observed, the separation process was protracted and painful.

How do you avoid getting to the point in a partnership when separation is the only reasonable option? The first step is to use the pre-partnership planning process we describe in part one. In the case of the rift between two of the UDEP partners, the lack of an honest, in-depth, getting-to-know-you period meant that seeds of conflict probably were present from the start and were never weeded out. As one of UDEP's key leaders said, "We would never have partnered had we known how incompatible we were on all levels, how different our theories of action were." The second step, once in a partnership, is to use the good practices described in this chapter and elsewhere in this book.

## Chapter Summary

> **Core Idea:** Trust is a vital component of partnership work, particularly in collaborative partnerships in which different affinity groups must work together closely toward a common goal. Leaders must develop trust carefully through strategies that include promoting group stability, encouraging face-to-face interactions, and actively managing power dynamics. When the inevitable conflicts emerge, leaders must deal with them quickly and turn conflict into an opportunity for growth and a renewed sense of purpose.

### *Dynamics of Trust in Partnership*

- When there is no trust, partnership is virtually impossible.
- Trust is developed once individuals and groups become predictable and dependable and can be assumed to operate in good faith.
- While a certain degree of trust is required in all types of partnership, it is absolutely essential in collaborative partnerships.
- Trust develops incrementally over time and must be nurtured by partnership leaders.

### *Strategies for Developing Trust*

- Establish predictability and stability within working groups, thus allowing individuals to become more comfortable with their new colleagues.
- Engage in many face-to-face interactions, which engender a sense of familiarity and collegiality among members of a group.
- Use progressive interactions to create an emotionally safe working environment.

- Engage with ground-floor workers at all points of the partnership to demonstrate to local stakeholders that you are taking pains to tailor the work to local realities.
- Surface and manage power dynamics.

## *Managing Conflict in Education Partnerships*

- Diagnose the type (e.g., interpersonal, intragroup) and nature (malevolent or benevolent) of the conflict. Try to avert or minimize the malevolent conflicts, which can wreak havoc on a partnership.
- Use established strategies for managing conflict.
- Build a foundation of trust; many conflicts can be weathered successfully if sufficient trust exists.
- Use conflict to provide a partnership with an opportunity to develop new, creative responses to problems and a sense of group identity.
- Use mediators to manage conflicts.
- Consider dissolving the partnership if the level of conflict becomes psychologically or programmatically harmful to individuals or organizations.

## Bibliographic Note

For an excellent discussion of conflict in collaborative work and many of the various options available to leaders in these situations, see Gray (2008) in *The Oxford Handbook of Inter-Organizational Relations.* The research on trust in collaborations and interorganizational relations is extensive; see Gray (1989), Ring and Van de Ven (1994), Rotter (1980), Thomson and Perry (2006), and Vangen and Huxham (2003) for an overview of the topic.

# EPILOGUE

I n 2010, partnerships constitute a core element of education reform strategy. The federal government, many states, private foundations, and
individual organizations have been turning to partnerships to deal with
entrenched challenges, such as college access, data alignment, and teacher
education. Whether public or private, these entities expect partnerships to
accomplish benefits that the partner organizations, alone, probably cannot
accomplish.

Twenty-two years have passed since Sirotnik and Goodlad's important
book, *School-University Partnerships in Action*, was published. In 1988, they
clearly recognized both the promises and challenges represented by
partnerships:

> We see the cup of potential for productive school-university partnerships
> to be at least half full. To be sure, developing and realizing this potential
> will not be without attendant problems and conflicts. (p. xii)

> Getting beyond turf problems, calcified reward structures, trivial agendas,
> already-full schedules, and regularities designed to keep things the way they
> are will not be easy. But the general pressure in the surrounding society for
> doing much better has rarely been stronger. . . . The opportunities for
> educational renewal are many. Among them, school-university partner-
> ships may be an idea whose time is come. (p. 224)

In their discussion of the challenges facing education partnerships, Sirotnik and Goodlad (1988) honed in on key issues that practitioners must contend with:

- merging cultures so as to achieve and maintain a productive tension;
- developing trust and ownership;

- treating change as a nonlinear process that requires flexibility; and
- developing a common agenda.

They also posed several principles of partnership work that would increase the opportunity for partnerships to successfully realize their goals:

- finding people who function as effective boundary crossers;
- establishing appropriate governance and organizational structures;
- making sure that the resources match the rhetoric;
- knitting together a common framework;
- making efficient use of time and avoiding running on parallel tracks;
- maintaining constant awareness of change and of change processes; and
- fostering institutional and individual renewal by celebrating success.

So where do things stand today? Partnership work has flourished and is a core feature of both federal- and state-level education policy, in large part due to the widely accepted view that the entire K–12 system must be engaged and connected to address the complex and entrenched challenges facing teaching and learning in our nation's K–12 schools and IHEs. As one anonymous reviewer of this book argued, "Democratic partnerships of universities, schools, and an array of neighborhood and community organizations are the most promising means of improving the lives of our nation's young people."

While examples of successful and effective partnerships abound, policy leaders and practitioners alike are coming to understand that partnership work is very challenging and should not be viewed as a panacea. Both successful and unsuccessful partnerships continue to experience a common set of challenges, from navigating cultural differences to obtaining high-quality data for demonstrating program efficacy and outcomes. A particular challenge is the need to develop and sustain initiatives as part of cohesive wholes. This approach contrasts with what one UDEP participant called "project-itis," whereby a K–12 district or an IHE engages in a series of projects that are weakly connected to a long-term view of systemic change.

We contend that enough evidence and knowledge has accumulated regarding education partnerships that we can begin to chart a way for practitioners to design and implement initiatives in a more informed and locally appropriate manner. Acting on this view, we focus in this book on the unique characteristics and constraints of every partnership and avoid providing overly proscriptive lists of best practices. Our view is that there is no easy road to partnership, no finite "to-do list" that will apply to every partnership in every situation. Indeed, Sirotnik and Goodlad (1988) voiced this same opinion by arguing that it is important not to "package and disseminate detailed models of how partnerships function best" (p. x). Furthermore, the evidence accumulated over the last 22 years indicates that Sirotnik and Goodlad got it right. The challenges in partnership work are adaptive, emergent, and context dependent, changing over time and in response to diverse organizational structures, resources, and personality types.

However, some common themes and principles characterize effective and successful partnership efforts. These include features reviewed in this book, among them boundary crossing, effective communication systems, and strong planning procedures. In light of these principles and the growing focus on systemic reform, we designed this book to give practitioners a diagnostic framework that is based on these principles and that enables identification of the various and interconnected moving parts of a partnership. Implicit in this framework is the metaphor of the 3rd space of partnership. This metaphor evokes the idea of an organizational entity that entails, yet is separate from, the existing web of established cultural entities in which it operates. Like these existing cultural entities—the insitutions and organizations contributing to the creation of the partnerships—the 3rd space you develop involves many complex cultural elements, such as communication styles, expectations, attitudes, legal and financial structures, and working practices. We hope this lens will allow you to view your own partnership work with more nuance, to enter into partnership more prepared for the inevitable challenges, and to design and manage your partnership with more intention and care. As you move ahead in your partnership work, we thus encourage you to pause and reflect whether you have considered the following overarching principles.

## Think of Organizations and Partnerships in Multifaceted Terms

Have you begun thinking of your own and your partners' organizations and suborganizations—as well as your 3rd space of partnership—in terms of their specific structure and technologies, cultural models, relationships, and routines and practices? Take a lesson from the cultural anthropologist Clifford Geertz (1973), who argued that to develop an adequate understanding of the dynamics of a culture a person must carefully observe and analyze many elements and develop a thick description (p. 6) of the culture. Essential to this process of developing a "thick description" in a partnership is to carefully identify the subcultures within your partner organizations that are relevant to your partnership. A "nuanced" knowledge of these cultural dynamics will help you to identify and navigate between and across the boundaries of all of the organizations involved in your partnership.

## Plan and Get Acquainted

Have you initiated a planning stage for the potential partnership? This planning stage isn't limited to learning about others. It also requires a close diagnosis of those attributes of your own organization that are relevant to establishing a partnership. Socrates' advice is still sound: "Know thyself." A careful understanding of your own organization will help you determine whether moving forward is in the best interests of all parties.

## Engage in a Careful Design Process

Have you engaged in a careful design process? Designing the new partnership entity is complicated by the fact that the preexisting needs and constraints of multiple organizations have to be considered when crafting these structures and procedures. The organizational structure of a partnership will guide decision making, task implementation, and administration, and if these features are at odds with the existing cultural dynamics of participants, a smoothly operating partnership is unlikely. Take the time, from the beginning, to design organizational structures and administrative procedures that fit the nature of your goals and objectives (e.g., technical or adaptive problems), the relevant "inherited" features of the partner organizations, and other aspects of your partnership.

## Emphasize Boundary Crossing

Once the partnership is designed, a key aspect of successful implementation is the presence of project personnel who are both flexible and able to cross organizational and cultural boundaries. Are you selecting leaders with, and also developing, these capacities? And given the unpredictable nature of partnerships, where events and conditions change all the time, are you identifying and developing people who can contend with unpredictable challenges, differences of opinion among the different participants, and the likely need to adapt to changing circumstances?

## Take Advantage of the Opportunity to Foster New Cultural Dynamics

Recall that the deeply held values and beliefs of a group, or their cultural models, are linked to specific structural features of an organization, relationships, and practices. Thus, you have the opportunity to create new task environments that will foster new structures, relationships, and practices, which, in turn, may generate new ways of thinking. Partnership work offers an opportunity to create a new organizational milieu for participants from a variety of backgrounds and organizations. It is up to you to craft this milieu in ways that encourage new modes of thinking and acting, as opposed to reinforcing regressive patterns. It is also important to recognize that conflict in partnership work presents opportunity, as conflict and cognitive dissonance are often necessary to move groups to explore new ideas and possibilities.

Based on research that we and others have conducted, we believe that by practicing these challenging principles, you will be better able to navigate diverse cultural contexts of partnership and turn the challenges of partnership into fulfilled promise.

# METHODOLOGY

I n this appendix, we briefly review the methods used in this study, including the design, setting and sample, data-collection procedures, and data analysis procedures. The research questions that informed each of these methods are: (1) What are the component parts of partnerships at different points in time? and (2) How do these factors interact to result in particular outcomes?

## Design

Given the focus on uncovering the constituent parts and processes of part-nership operations, we decided a case-study design was most appropriate (Merriam, 1998). Case studies are particularly useful because they help researchers conduct empirical inquiry into a "contemporary phenomenon within its real life context, especially when the boundaries between phenom-enon and context are not clearly evident" (Yin, 2003, p. 23). Additionally, we structured this study as an embedded design because it focuses on two different units of analysis: the partnership as a whole and four distinct work-ing groups. Finally, the design is also a multisite case study, which increases the opportunity to identify patterns across cases. In multisite case studies, multiple cases are analyzed using the same methods to find either contradic-tory or corroborating evidence from two or more cases.

## Setting and Sample

The partnership analyzed in this study was part of a national program to improve math and science education for students in the nation's K–12 schools by establishing partnerships among science, technology, engineering, and mathematics (STEM) faculty; education faculty; and K–12 administra-tors and teachers. In this book, we use a pseudonym, the Urban District

Education Partnership (UDEP), to describe the partnership we studied. Funded for five years, the UDEP partnership sought to improve mathematics and science teaching and learning in urban areas by bringing about organizational changes in participating school districts and institutions of higher education (IHEs). As noted, the units of analysis for this study were the partnership as a whole and four distinct working groups. The criteria for working groups were that the group (1) have responsibility for accomplishing one or more tasks intended to help achieve one or more of the partnership's goals, (2) have at least two members who represented different organizations (or administrative units from the same organization), and (3) meet at least three times to chart its progress. The groups selected were identified by key participants of the project as being the most active and long-lasting working groups of the UDEP. The groups were the following:

- The senior leadership group: This team, which consisted of leaders from each of the partners, was to provide overall management and vision for the entire project. The senior leadership team became increasingly dysfunctional and evolved into separate leadership teams centered at two of the IHEs.
- A preservice (i.e., future K–12 teachers) math group based in an IHE: This committee consisted of faculty and doctoral students from the mathematics department and an education department at one of the IHEs and representatives from the local district. The group focused on revising a sequence of math courses for future elementary and middle school teachers.
- A science professional-development group based in a district: This group consisted of education and science faculty from two IHEs, representatives from the local district, and professional-development consultants from another IHE. The group focused on developing a series of science professional-development workshops for K–12 teachers in a large urban district.
- A math professional-development group based in a district: This group consisted of the members of one district's math leadership group guided by leaders from one of the IHEs. This group began operating as part of a district/IHE initiative, which began before the UDEP grant was funded.

Subjects were selected using a purposive and snow-ball sampling procedure, and respondents included program administrators, university faculty and academic staff, and K–12 district administrators and teachers ($N = 50$).

It is important to note that some of these individuals participated in more than one working group, which explains why the number of respondents included in the analyses at the working group level exceed the total sample amount. In these instances, a single interview included information about more than one working group, so a single interview was included in more than one working group data set. The interviews followed the ethnographic interview method developed by James Spradley (1979), in which the interviewer uses a semistructured protocol but also focuses on eliciting native terminology and the respondents' interests to guide the line of questioning. A team of three analysts conducted interviews with 50 individuals at three points in time over the course of four years (Year 1, Year 3, and Year 5). Given the high rate of turnover in these working groups, some participants were interviewed only at one point, while others were interviewed at two or three points, thus yielding a total of 62 interviews conducted for this study. In instances where an individual was interviewed multiple times, that person's separate transcripts were collapsed into a single transcript file for analysis. The interviews lasted between 45 minutes and two hours, and were digitally recorded and transcribed.

The analytic methods used in the study include a combination of a structured approach to grounded theory to categorize data, and causal network analysis (CNA) to identify links among these data points was deemed the most suitable. All interview transcript files were processed by NVivo qualitative data analysis software, and the resulting data were reduced and categorized. The analysts used a structured approach to grounded theory to accomplish data reduction and categorization. This approach differs from other grounded theory in that it uses a "coding paradigm" from the beginning of the analytic process to analyze the data, as opposed to a completely inductive approach to developing a coding scheme (Strauss & Corbin, 1990).

A coding scheme was developed that combined elements from the conceptual framework as well as inductively derived categories from the data. Using a subsample of 14 interviews with key informants (i.e., principal participants or leaders), a team of three analysts identified several key aspects of partnership formation and operations for three points in time: antecedent or preexisting conditions, process or implementation, and outcomes. These themes constituted the subcategories under each of the primary cultural dynamics factors. In this way, the classification system included terms that were identified both inductively and deductively. This classification scheme was then used to create four separate master data lists (MDLs) for each working group. Each of these documents listed each of the coding categories for the three time periods. Then all of the data fragments were sorted into a separate MDL for each working group. One point that bears elaboration here is that the cultural model category is subsumed under the sociocultural factor header. To identify cultural models, following a convention in cognitive anthropology, at least three individuals had to express the same belief, value, or view, which was found in the individual experiences category.

The next step was to establish relationships among these data points. CNA is often used to identify relationships between specific data points to organize complex data in a more coherent manner (Miles & Huberman, 1994). The method involves taking data points that are organized temporally, and identifying relationships among these data through time. The analysts reviewed the MDL data and first identified key partnership outcomes as claimed by individuals (e.g., the creation of new curricula or the dissolution of the partnership), and then worked backward to identify what process and antecedent conditions the individual cited as contributing to the outcome. In some cases the respondent explicitly identified relationships between factors (e.g., effective leadership led to successful group outcomes). In other cases the analyst inferred the relationship from the data. These relations were then placed into what are called causal fragments, and 256 of these were identified across all of the groups: senior leadership group (107), preservice math group (52), science professional-development group (59), and math professional-development group (38). The next stage of the analysis involved grouping each fragment thematically across individuals within a given working group. For instance, four different fragments from individuals within the same working group regarding how using e-mail led to group dysfunction would be clustered together as a single theme and given a label. This resulted in the following thematic groupings: senior leadership group (28), preservice math group (11), science professional-development group (13), and math professional-development group (9). Finally, each of the working groups' themes was placed into a data table for the entire partnership, which enabled a comparative analysis across each working group.

As this book is not a straightforward reporting of these data sources, we feel compelled to note how we arrived at the principles of partnership that form the core of the book. The process of deriving actionable information from a large and complex set of data is aptly described by Jim Collins in his description of the methodology used to write his 2001 book, *Good to Great*:

> The best answer I can give is that it was an iterative process of looping back and forth, developing ideas and testing them against the data, revising

the ideas, building a framework, seeing it break under the weight of evidence, and rebuilding it yet again. That process was repeated over and over, until everything held together in a coherent framework of concepts. (p. 11)

We found that this explanation accurately described our research process as well. In addition the analysts achieved reliability for the analytic procedures through frequent research team meetings, in-depth discussions about analytic decisions, trial coding runs and subsequent code scheme revisions, and triangulation among data sources (Miles & Huberman, 1994). In particular, decision rules played an important role, and these are clearly stated criteria used by qualitative researchers to make coding or other analytic decisions, which are critical to improve the transparency and robustness of qualitative research (Miles & Huberman, 1994). Limitations to this study include the lack of generalizability due to the analysis of a single case and, turnover in the research team over the course of the project.

# REFERENCES

Accenture. (1999). *Dispelling the myths of alliances.* Retrieved from http://www.ac centure.com/Global/Research_and_Insights/Outlook/By_Alphabet/ DispellingAlliances.htm

Agar, M. (1996). *The professional stranger: An informal introduction to ethnography.* San Diego, CA: Academic Press.

Aldrich, H., & Herker, D. (1977). Boundary spanning roles and organization structure. *The Academy of Management Review, 2*(2), 217–230.

Amey, M. J., Eddy, P. L., & Ozaki, C. C. (2007). Demands for partnerships and collaboration in higher education: A model. In M. J. Amey (Ed.), *Collaborations across educational borders* (pp. 5–16). New Directions for Community Colleges No. 139. San Francisco: Jossey-Bass.

Anderson, H., & Helms, J. V. (2001). The ideal of standards and the reality of schools: Needed research. *Journal of Research in Science Teaching, 38*(1), 3–16.

Austin, A. E. (1996). Institutional and departmental cultures: The relationship between teaching and research. *New Directions for Institutional Research, 84,* 65–82.

Axelrod, R., & Cohen, M. D. (2000). *Harnessing complexity: Organizational implications of a scientific frontier.* New York: Free Press.

Barringer, B. R., & Harrison, J. S. (2000). Walking a tightrope: Creating value through interorganizational relationships. *Journal of Management, 26*(3), 367–403.

Becher, T., & Trowler, P. (2003). *Academic tribes and territories* (2nd ed.). Philadelphia: Open University Press.

Bennis, W. (1994). *Flight plan for leaders.* Los Angeles: University of Southern California Business School.

Birnbaum, R. (1991). *How colleges work: The cybernetics of academic organizations and leadership.* San Francisco: Jossey-Bass.

Borthwick, A. C. (2001). Dancing in the dark? Learning more about what makes partnerships work. In R. Ravid & M. Handler (Eds.), *The many faces of school-university collaborations* (pp. 23–41). Englewood, CO: Libraries Unlimited.

Boulding, K. (1962). *Conflict and defense: A general theory.* New York: Harper & Brothers.

Brown, J. S., Collins, A., & Duguid, P. (1989). Situated cognition and the culture of learning. *Educational Researcher, 18*(1), 32–42.

Burt, R. S. (1992). *Structural holes: The social structure of competition.* Cambridge, MA: Harvard University Press.

California Alliance of Pre K–18 Partnerships. (2004). *Raising student achievement through effective education partnerships: Policy and practice.* Long Beach, CA: California Academic Partnerships Program.

Center for the Advancement of Collaborative Strategies in Health. (2010). Retrieved from http://www.cacsh.org

Clark, B. R. (1972). The organizational saga in higher education. *Administrative Science Quarterly, 17*(2), 178–184.

Clark, R. W. (1988). School-university relationships: An interpretive review. In K. A. Sirotnik & J. I. Goodlad (Eds.), *School-university partnerships in action: Concepts, cases, and concerns* (pp. 32–65). New York: Teachers College Press.

Clark, R. W. (1999a). *Effective professional development schools.* San Francisco: Jossey-Bass.

Clark, R. W. (1999b). School-university partnerships and professional development schools. *Peabody Journal of Education, 74*(3&4), 164–177.

Clifford, J., & Marcus, G. E. (1986). *Writing culture: The poetics and politics and ethnography.* Los Angeles: University of California Press.

Clifford, M., & Millar, S. (2008). *K–20 partnerships: Literature review and recommendations for research.* Wisconsin Center for Education Research Working Paper Series (2008-3). Madison: University of Wisconsin.

Coburn, C. E. (2001). Collective sensemaking about reading: How teachers mediate reading policy in their professional communities. *Educational Evaluation and Policy Analysis, 23*(2), 145–170.

Cole, M., & Engestrom, Y. (1993). A cultural-historical approach to distributed cognition. In G. Salomon (Ed.), *Distributed cognitions: Psychological and educational considerations* (pp. 1–46). New York: Cambridge University Press.

Collins, J. (2001). *Good to great: Why some companies make the leap, and others don't.* New York: Harper Business.

Cyert, R. M., & Goodman, P. S. (1997). Creating effective university-industry alliances: An organizational learning perspective. *Organizational Dynamics, 25*(4), 45–57.

D'Andrade, R. (1995). *The development of cognitive anthropology.* Cambridge, UK: Cambridge University Press.

Davis, K. S., Feldman, A., Irwin, C., Pedevillano, E. D., Weiss, T., Bray, P. M., et al. (2003). Wearing the letter jacket: Legitimate participation in a collaborative science, mathematics, engineering, and technology education reform project. *School Science and Mathematics, 103,* 121–135.

Deloitte & Touche. (2009). Retrieved from http://www.deloitte.com/view/en_US/us/Services/audit-enterprise-risk-services/index.htm

Derry, S. J., DaCosta, M. C., Hmelo-Silver, C. E., et al. (2000). Toward assessment of knowledge-building practices in technology-mediated work group interactions. In S. P. Lajoie (Ed.), *Computers as cognitive tools: Volume 1, No more walls* (pp. 29–68). Mahwah, NJ: Erlbaum.

DiMaggio, P. (1997). Culture and cognition. *Annual Review of Sociology, 23*, 263–288.

DiMaggio, P., & Powell, W. (1983). The iron cage revisited: Institutional isomorphism and collective rationality in organizational fields. *American Sociological Review, 48*, 147–160.

Fried, J., & Hansson, D. H. (2010). *Rework.* New York: Crown Business.

Fullan, M. (2001). *The new meaning of educational change* (3rd ed.). New York: Teachers College Press.

Gamoran, A., et al. (2003). *Transforming teaching in math and science: How school districts can support change.* New York: Teachers College Press.

Gee, J. P. (2007). *What video games have to teach us about learning and literacy* (2nd ed.). New York: Palgrave Macmillan.

Geertz, C. (1973). The interpretation of cultures. New York: Basic Books.

Goffman, E. (1974). *Frame analysis: An essay on the organization of experience.* New York: Harper & Row.

Goleman, D. (1995). *Emotional intelligence.* New York: Bantam Books.

Granovetter, M. S. (1973). The strength of weak ties. *American Journal of Sociology, 78*(6), 1360–1380.

Gray, B. (1989). *Collaborating: Finding common ground for multiparty problems.* San Francisco: Jossey-Bass.

Gray, B. (2008). Intervening to improve interorganizational partnerships. In S. Cropper, M. Ebers, C. Huxham, & P. S. Ring (Eds.), *The Oxford handbook of inter-organizational relations* (pp. 664–690). New York: Oxford University Press.

Greeno, J. G. (1998). The situativity of knowing, learning, and research. *American Psychologist, 53*(1), 5–26.

Gutierrez, K. P., Baquedano-Lopez, P., & Tejada, C. (1999). Rethinking diversity: Hybridity and hybrid language practices in the 3rd space. *Mind, Culture, and Activity, 6*(4), 268–303.

Halverson, R. (2003). Systems of practice: How leaders use artifacts to create professional community in schools. *Education Policy Analysis Archives, 11*, 37–72.

Hamm, J. (2006, May). The five messages leaders must manage. *Harvard Business Review,* 2–10.

Heath, C., & Heath, D. (2007). *Made to stick: Why some ideas survive and others die.* New York: Random House.

Heifitz, R. A. (1994). *Leadership without easy answers.* Cambridge, MA: Harvard University Press.

Hodgkinson, H. L. (1999). *All one system: A second look.* Washington, DC: Institute for Educational Leadership, Inc.

Holmes, J. G., & Rempel, J. K. (1989). Trust in close relationships. In C. Hendrick (Ed.), *Review of Personality and Social Psychology, Vol. 10.* Beverly Hills, CA: Sage.

Hora, M. T., Millar, S. B., Arrigoni, J., & Kretchmar, K. (2009). *The challenges of producing evidence-based claims: An exploratory study of the NSF's Math and Science Partnership Community.* Wisconsin Center for Education Research Working Paper 2009-4. Madison: University of Wisconsin.

Houck, J. W., Cohn, C. K., & Cohn, C. A. (Eds.). (2004). *Partnering to lead educational renewal: High-quality teachers, high-quality schools.* New York: Teachers College Press.

Huber, G. P. (1991). Organizational learning: The contributing processes and the literature. *Organization Science, 2*(1), 88–115.

Intriligator, B. (1982). Interorganizational collaboration: A strategy for faculty development and organizational renewal. *Journal of Teacher Education, 33*(5), 14–17.

Intriligator, B. (1992, April). *Establishing interorganizational structures that facilitate successful school partnerships.* Paper presented at the annual meeting of the American Educational Research Association, San Francisco.

Johnston, M. (1997). *Contradictions in collaboration: New thinking on school/university partnerships.* New York: Teachers College Press.

Katzenmeyer, C., & Lawrenz, F. (2006). National Science Foundation perspectives on the nature of STEM program evaluation. *New Directions for Evaluation, 109,* 7–18.

Keating, P. J., & Clark, R. W. (1988). Accent on leadership: The Puget Sound Educational Consortium. In K. A. Sirotnik & J. I. Goodlad (Eds.), *School-university partnerships in action: Concepts, cases, and concerns* (pp. 148–166). New York: Teachers College Press.

Kezar, A., & Eckel, P. (2002). The effect of institutional culture on change strategies in higher education: Universal principles or culturally responsive concepts? *The Journal of Higher Education, 73*(4), 435–460.

Kingsley, G. (2005). Invited presentation on education partnership. Madison: University of Wisconsin.

Kirschner, B., Dickinson, R., & Blosser, C. (1996). From co-operation to collaboration: The changing culture of a school/university partnership. *Theory Into Practice, 35,* 205–213.

Kluckhohn, C. (1949). *Mirror for man.* New York: Whittlesey House.

Labaree, D. F. (2006). *The trouble with ed schools.* New Haven, CT: Yale University Press.

Lave, J. (1988). *Cognition in practice.* New York: Cambridge University Press.

Linden, R. M. (2002). *Working across boundaries: Making collaboration work in government and nonprofit organizations.* San Francisco: Jossey-Bass.

Locke, E. A., & Latham, G. P. (2002). Building a practically useful theory of goal setting and task motivation: A 35-year odyssey. *American Psychologist, 57*(9), 705–717.

March, J. G. (1991). Exploration and exploitation in organizational learning. *Organization Science, 2*(1), 71–87.

Martin, J. (2002). *Organizational culture: Mapping the terrain.* Thousand Oaks, CA: Sage.

Mattessich, P. W., Murray-Close, M., & Monsey, B. R. (2001). *Collaboration: What makes it work: A review of research literature on factors influencing successful collaboration* (2nd ed.). St. Paul, MN: Amherst H. Wilder Foundation.

Merriam, S. B. (1998). *Qualitative research and case study applications in education.* San Francisco: Jossey-Bass.

Miles, M. B., & Huberman, A. M. (1994). *Qualitative data analysis* (2nd ed.). Thousand Oaks, CA: Sage.

Mintzberg, H., Dougherty, O., Jorgensen, J., & Westley, F. (1996). Some surprising things about collaboration—knowing how people connect makes it work better. *Organizational Dynamics, 25*(1), 60–72.

Mitchell, S. (Ed.). (2002). *Effective educational partnerships: Experts, advocates, and scouts.* Westport, CT: Praeger.

Mohr, J., & Spekman, R. (1994). Characteristics of partnership success: Partnership attributes, communication behavior, and conflict resolution techniques. *Strategic Management Journal, 15,* 135–152.

Morgan, G. (1998). *Images of organization* (2nd ed.). Thousand Oaks, CA: Sage.

Narayan, S. (2009, July 19). Corner Office. *New York Times,* p. BU2.

National Research Council. (2000). *How people learn: Brain, mind, experience, and school.* Washington, DC: National Research Council.

Nisbet, M. C., & Mooney, C. (2007). Framing science. *Science, 316*(5821), 56.

Oliver, C. (1990). Determinants of interorganizational relations: Integration and future directions. *The Academy of Management Review, 15*(2), 241–265.

Ostrom, E. (1998). A behavioral approach to the Rational Choice Theory of Collective Action. *American Political Science Review, 92*(1), 1–22.

O'Sullivan, R. G. (2004). *Practicing evaluation: A collaborative approach.* Thousand Oaks, CA: Sage.

Owens, R. G. (2001). *Organizational behavior in education: Instructional leadership and school reform* (7th ed.). Needham Heights, MA: Allyn & Bacon.

Patton, M. Q. (2006, October). Paper presented at the MSP Evaluation Summit II: Using Evaluation Data to Communicate Findings, Minneapolis, MN.

Patton, M. Q. (2008). *Utilization-focused evaluation* (4th ed.). Thousand Oaks, CA: Sage.

Parker, B., & Selsky, J. W. (2004). Interface dynamics in cause-based partnerships: An exploration of emergent culture. *Nonprofit and Voluntary Sector Quarterly, 33*(3), 458–488.

Perkins, D. (2003). *King Arthur's round table: How collaborative conversations create smart organizations.* Hoboken, NJ: John Wiley & Sons.

Ravid, R., & Handler, M. G. (2001). *The many faces of school-university collaboration: Characteristics of successful partnerships.* Englewood, CO: Teacher Ideas Press.

Resnick, L. B., Besterfield-Sacre, M., Mehalik, M. M., Sherar, J. Z., Halverson, E. R. (2007). A framework for effective management of school system performance. In P. A. Moss (Ed.), *Evidence and decision making. The 106th Yearbook of the National Society for the Study of Education* (NSS), Part 1 (pp. 155–185). Malden, MA: Blackwell.

Ring, P. S., & Van de Ven, A. H. (1994). Developmental processes of cooperative interorganizational relationships. *Academy of Management Journal, 19*(1), 90–118.

Rotter, J. B. (1980). Interpersonal trust, trustworthiness, and gullibility. *American Psychologist, 35,* 1–7.

Schmidt, S. M., & Kuchan, T. A. (1977). Interorganizational relationships: Patterns and motivations. *Administrative Science Quarterly, 22*(2), 22–37.

Seely Brown, J., et al. (2005). *Storytelling in organizations: Why storytelling is transforming 21st century organizations and management.* Burlington, MA: Elsevier Butterworth Heinemann.

Seely Brown, J., & Duguid, P. (2002). *The social life of information.* Boston: Harvard Business School Press.

Senge, P. (1994). *The fifth discipline: The art and practice of the learning organization.* New York: Doubleday Business.

Sirotnik, K. A., & Goodlad, J. I. (Eds.). (1988). *School-university partnerships in action: Concepts, cases, and concerns.* New York: Teachers College Press.

Siskin, L. S. S. (1991). Departments as different worlds: Subject subcultures in secondary schools. *Educational Administration Quarterly, 27*(2), 134–160.

Slater, L. (2004). Collaboration: A framework for school improvement. *International Electronic Journal for Leadership in Learning, 8*(5). Retrieved from http://www.u calgary.ca/iejll/vol8/Slater

Spillane, J. P., & Diamond, J. B. (Eds.). (2007). *Distributed leadership in practice.* New York: Teachers College Press.

Spillane, J., Reiser, B., & Reimer, T. (2002). Policy implementation and cognition: Reframing and refocusing implementation research. *Review of Educational Research, 72*(3), 387–431.

Spradley, J. (1979). *The ethnographic interview.* New York: Holt, Rinehart & Winston.

Stajkovic, A., Locke, E. A., & Blair, E. S. (2006). A first examination of the relationships between primed subconscious goals, assigned conscious goals, and task performance. *Journal of Applied Psychology, 91*(5), 1172–1180.

Strauss, C., & Corbin, J. (1990). *Basics of qualitative research: Techniques and procedures for developing grounded theory* (3rd ed.). Thousand Oaks, CA: Sage.

Strauss, C., & Quinn, N. (1997). *A cognitive theory of cultural meaning.* Cambridge, UK: Cambridge University Press.

Teitel, L. (1998). Separations, divorces, and open marriages in professional development school partnerships. *Journal of Teacher Education, 49*(2), 85–96.

Thain, D., Tannenbaum, T., & Livny, M. (2005). Distributed computing in practice: The Condor experience. *Concurrency and Computation: Practice and Experience, 17,* 323–356.

Thomson, A. M., & Perry, J. L. (2006). Collaboration process: Inside the black box. *Public Administration Review, 66*(1), 20–32.

Tierney, W. G. (2008). *The impact of culture on organizational decision making: Theory and practice in higher education.* Sterling, VA: Stylus.

Tsui, A., Edwards, G., & Lopez-Real, F. (2009). *Learning in school-university partnerships: Sociocultural perspectives.* New York: Routledge.

Tsui, A., & Law, D. (2007). Learning as boundary-crossing in school-university partnership. *Teaching and Teacher Education, 23,* 1289–1301.

Tuckman, B. W., & Jensen, M. A. C. (1977). Stages of small group development revisited. *Group and Organization Studies, 2*(4), 419–427.

Tushnet, N. C. (1993). *A guide to developing educational partnerships.* Washington, DC: Office of Educational Research and Improvement. (ERIC Document Reproduction Service No. ED362992).

Vangen, S., & Huxham, C. (2003). Nurturing collaborative relations: Building trust in interorganizational collaborations. *Journal of Applied Behavioral Science, 39*(5), 5–31.

Waschak, M., & Kingsley, G. (2006). *Education partnerships: Defining, observing, measuring and evaluating.* Working paper. Atlanta, GA: School of Public Policy, Georgia Institute of Technology.

Weick, K. E. (1976). Educational organizations as loosely coupled systems. *Administrative Science Quarterly, 21*(1), 1–19.

Whetten, D. A. (1981). Interorganizational relations: A review of the field. *Journal of Higher Education, 52*(1), 1–28.

Wilkof, M., Brown, D., & Selsky, J. (1995). When the stories are different: The influence of corporate culture mismatches on interorganizational relations. *Journal of Applied Behavioral Science, 31*(3), 373–388.

Williams, P. (2002). The competent boundary spanner. *Public Administration, 80*(1), 103–124.

Wolcott, H. (1997). Ethnographic research in education. In R. M. Jaeger (Ed.), *Complementary methods for research in education* (pp. 327–353). Washington, DC: American Educational Research Association.

Yin, R. K. (2003). *Case study research, design and methods* (3rd ed.). Newbury Park, CA: Sage.

# GLOSSARY

**Adaptive expertise:** The ability of an individual to apply skills and knowledge to novel problems and situations.

**Adaptive problem:** A problem that even the best experts have not clearly defined, let alone solved. Adaptive problems require innovation and creativity, and probably will take a long time to address adequately.

**Affinity groups:** People who share a particular craft or set of interests, and who occupy similar niches or roles within an organization.

**Autonomy:** The quality of being self-directing or self-governing.

**Black box:** A metaphor for a system that is viewed only in terms of inputs and outputs, without insights into its internal mechanisms.

**Boundary crosser:** An individual who works across organizational and cultural boundaries effectively. A boundary crosser may or may not be in a leadership position.

**Co-construction:** The process whereby two or more individuals work collaboratively to create a new product, policy, or procedure.

**Collaborative partnership:** A partnership structure that is tightly coupled and uses a consensus-based governance system.

**Contact architecture:** An organization's communication infrastructure that creates occasions and roles through which people connect and interact.

**Coordinated partnership:** A partnership structure that uses a horizontal system with no centralized governance system.

**Cultural dynamics:** A multifaceted view of culture in organizations that accounts for cultural models, structure and technologies, relationships, and routines and practices; together these factors interact and constitute the cultural dynamics in a single organization or partnership.

**Cultural model:** A deeply ingrained set of beliefs and/or knowledge that is widely shared among members of a group.

**Distributed leadership:** A type of leadership practice that emphasizes the interaction of leaders, followers, and the situation, and that depends on leadership being distributed among many people, each of whom is embedded in specific organizational contexts rather than in the actions of "hero leaders."

**Embedded relationships:** Preexisting relationships and interactions.

**Formative evaluation:** A type of evaluation used to monitor program implementation and progress. Data from formative evaluations can be used to improve program activities midstream and ensure that the program is unfolding according to plan.

**Goal:** A projected state of affairs that a person or an organization hopes to realize in the future.

**Governance:** The activity of governing and making decisions. In organizations, management and administrative processes for a given area of responsibility can be considered a governance system.

**Home organization:** The organization to which people involved in a partnership report or have primary identification and affiliation with.

**Key informant:** An individual who provides critical information about a local situation, group, or organization. In ethnographic research a key informant is often an individual whom the researcher befriends, and who acts as a key source of information about a specific cultural group's way of life.

**Limited partnership:** A partnership structure where one organization clearly directs the actions of others, and a top-down governance system is in place.

**Mental model:** A psychological construct for interpreting the world and responding to new information, which is encoded and stored in long-term memory.

**Message framing:** How a theme or an issue is presented to the public so particular cues are activated in the audience's minds (see **Mental model**).

**Objective:** Specific steps or strategies that are projected to achieve a partnership's goals.

**Partnership:** An organization that is formed through an agreement among partners, comprising entities such as IHEs, school districts, and government agencies, and intended to produce benefits that the partners alone could not accomplish.

**Pre-partnership planning group:** A group comprising representatives from different organizations who convene to discuss the goals, objectives, and activities of the potential partnership prior to implementation.

**Preservice teacher education:** The training provided to student teachers before they have undertaken any teaching in the classroom.

**Progressive interactions:** Interactions among people that facilitate effective conveyance of information and generate positive feelings among participants.

**Relationships:** The social and professional ties and connections among individuals, groups, or organizations.

**Routine expertise:** Highly developed skills and knowledge that are applied to predictable, everyday problems.

**Routines and practices:** The specific acts and behaviors that individuals or groups engage in to carry out their work.

**Structure and technology:** The policies, administrative procedures, and physical infrastructure (especially communication technology) that characterize an organization.

**Summative evaluation:** An evaluation focused on obtaining evidence of the ultimate outcomes or effects of a project.

**Technical problem:** A technical problem is one that, while perhaps very complex and difficult, experts know how to identify, define, and solve.

**Third (3rd) space:** The new and continually evolving arena for activity where competing interests and perspectives play out as different organizations come together.

**Working group:** A group that has responsibility for accomplishing one or more tasks to help achieve one or more of a partnership's goals, has at least two members who represent different organizations (or administrative units from the same organization), and meets at least three times to make progress on its tasks.

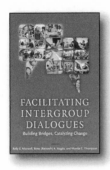

**Facilitating Intergroup Dialogues**
*http://stylus.styluspub.com/Books/BookDetail.aspx?productID=173146*
*Bridging Differences, Catalyzing Change*
Kelly E. Maxwell, Biren (Ratnesh) Nagda andMonita C. Thompson
Foreword by Patricia Gurin

Intergroup dialogue has emerged as an effective educational and community building method to bring together members of diverse social and cultural groups to engage in learning together so that they may work collectively and individually to promote greater diversity, equality and justice.

"This book is a treasure trove of theory, research, and personal narratives of both successes and challenges. Anyone interested in developing an intergroup dialogue program, or using the intergroup dialogue method in other courses, campus organizations, research labs, or other educational settings composed of people from diverse backgrounds will find this book their most important resource. So, too, will practitioners who work with diverse groups of people in communities and in state, national, and international organizations."—*Patricia Gurin*, *Nancy Cantor Distinguished University Professor Emerita of Psychology and Women's Studies, University of Michigan*

**Transforming Teacher Education**
*http://stylus.styluspub.com/Books/BookDetail.aspx?productID=219453*
*What Went Wrong with Teacher Training, and How We Can Fix It*
Edited by Valerie Hill-Jackson and Chance W. Lewis
Foreword by Peter McLaren

*"Why are fifteen million children and youth in poverty not achieving when we know that low-income students excel in the classrooms of "star" teachers (who comprise approximately 8 percent of the teaching force)?"*

*"Whose needs or interests are being met in education reform today?"*

*"In my own institution, there has not been a systematic assessment of the effectiveness of the basic teacher education program since the institution was founded over a century ago as a teachers college. Imagine, not one ever!"*

"This volume is the one of most comprehensive and deeply analytical works on teacher preparation to appear in decades. As a teacher educator, I deeply appreciate this thoughtful and critical examination of the issues, dilemmas, and trenchant problems of teaching and teacher education in America. This is a work well worth reading!"—*Peter C. Murrell, Jr.*, *Founding Dean, School of Education, and Professor of Educational Psychology , Loyola University Maryland*

22883 Quicksilver Drive
Sterling, VA 20166-2102

Subscribe to our e-mail alerts: www.Styluspub.com

# Also available from Stylus

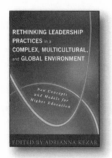

### Rethinking Leadership in a Complex, Multicultural, and Global Environment
*http://stylus.styluspub.com/Books/BookDetail.aspx?productID=171941*
*New Concepts and Models for Higher Education*
Edited by Adrianna Kezar

"Adrianna Kezar breaks new ground in this edited volume that focuses much-needed attention on the theory and practice of leadership in higher education. Trenchant analyses by leadership developers and scholars offer key insights on programmatic innovations that are responsive to rapidly evolving organizational environments in American colleges and universities. Their chapters provide readers with a user-friendly text for use in leadership development programs and for advancing the study of leadership in higher education. The exemplars of programs with proven track records as well as recommendations for "case-in-point" approaches to leadership development provide what Kezar refers to as "revolutionary" forms of leadership that emphasize empowerment, collaboration, social responsibility, cross-cultural understanding, and cognitive complexity. This book will be of interest to faculty, administrators, and leadership scholars concerned with the context and process of learning leadership in 21st century institutions."—*Judith Glazer-Raymo*, *Lecturer, Department of Higher & Postsecondary Education, Teachers College, Columbia University*

### The Impact of Culture on Organizational Decision-Making
*http://stylus.styluspub.com/Books/BookDetail.aspx?productID=172955*
*Theory and Practice in Higher Education*
William G. Tierney

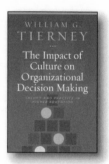

"The clear prose and cogent explanations certainly clarify how one's theory of organizational culture matters."—*Journal of College Student Retention*

"Tierney's call to look beyond the structures of large American research institutions and utilize a cultural model to understand organizational decision making should be a wake-up call to college and university administrators who wish to lead their organizations to success and excellence in the 21st century."—*Jim Mello*, *Assistant Provost for Financial Planning, University of Hartford*